West Ham United in the League Cup

1960 - 2011

John Northcutt

A *SoccerData* Publication

Best Wishes
John Northcutt

Published in Great Britain by Tony Brown,
4 Adrian Close, Beeston, Nottingham NG9 6FL.
Telephone 0115 973 6086. E-mail soccer@innotts.co.uk
First published 2011

Cover design by Bob Budd.

Printed and bound by 4Edge, Hockley, Essex
www.4edge.co.uk

ISBN: 978-1-905891-47-4

AUTHOR'S INTRODUCTION

The Football League Cup began in 1960-61 when West Ham beat Charlton 3-1 on the 26th September 1960. This was my first season as a regular at Upton Park and being a young schoolboy my pocket money would be spent on attending the league games. So I decided not to attend that particular Monday evening match, also thinking that this new League Cup competition would not last. Little did I know that over 50 years later it would still be competed for, although not perhaps as popular as the F.A. Cup. I look back with affection to those games in the 1960s, a time before millionaire footballers, spiralling ticket costs and all seated stadiums lacking atmosphere.

Going back to that first Hammers side there was full back John Lyall, who went on to become arguably West Ham's best ever manager. At wing-half was a young Bobby Moore, who within six years would hold the World Cup in his hands. In the passage of time sadly six of that team including all three-goal scorers have since died.

Despite the Hammers reaching 7 semi-finals and 2 finals they have never been able to win the Football League Cup. Their record in the competition however has been quite good, having lost only 56 matches of the 198 played.

Over the years there have been many memorable highlights to saviour. In 1965 Cardiff City were beaten in the semi-final with an aggregate score of 10-3. The mighty Leeds United were crushed 7-0 at Upton Park in 1966. A Geoff Hurst hat-trick in 1968 against Bolton Wanderers saw them thrashed 7-2. There was a League Cup record score attained in 1983 when the luckless Bury came to London and lost 10-0. A Paul Ince inspired Hammers knocked out Liverpool in 1988 with a 4-1 scoreline. Holders Manchester United were well beaten 4-0 in November 2010.

Of course, there have also been a few cup shocks along the way, including defeats by Darlington, Stockport County, Crewe, Northampton and Chesterfield. Not forgetting as well, a 6-0 defeat at Oldham in the 1990 semi-final.

All the match details are included in the book and I trust that they will bring back a host of memories from the past 50 years. All Hammers supporters will be hoping that the trophy will soon bear the claret and blue ribbons of West Ham United.

John Northcutt
March 2011

CONTENTS

Main section:

Appendices:

1960/61

Round One 26th September 1960

West Ham United 3 (Dick, Musgrove, Moore), Charlton Athletic 1 (Leary).
Att: 12,496. Referee: F Clarke.
West Ham United: Rhodes, Bond, Lyall, Malcolm, Brown, Moore, Woodley, Cartwright, Dunmore, Dick, Musgrove.
Charlton Athletic: Duff, Sewell, Townsend, Hinton, Tocknell, Lucas, Lawrie, Edwards, Leary, Werge, Summers.

The Hammers made their initial entry into the new Football League Cup competition but only 12,465 fans turned up to see this London derby. The Second Division side Charlton were on top in the opening stages and it was no surprise when Leary gave them the lead on 16 minutes. Andy Malcolm put through a long ball to Johnny Dick who pounced to score after 24 minutes. Thus Dick went into the record books as the club's first ever League Cup goalscorer.

In the second half West Ham gradually got on top and Malcolm Musgrove scored on 48 minutes after a slip by Hinton. It was left to Bobby Moore to finish the scoring when his volley hit the net in the 64th minute.

Round Two 24th October 1960

Darlington 3 (Spencer, Rayment, Robson), West Ham United 2 (Dunmore, Dick).
Att: 16,911. Referee: M Dixon.
Darlington: Tinsley, Henderson, Mulholland, Furphy, Greener, Spencer, Rayment, Milner, Robson, Baxter, Morton.
West Ham United: Rhodes, Bond, Lyall, Malcolm, Brown, Moore, Grice, Woosnam, Dunmore, Dick, Musgrove.

Darlington's biggest crowd of the season 17,057 roared on their favourites as they humbled First Division West Ham. The Hammers were rocked after only 30 seconds when Baxter turned the ball to Spence who crashed it in from 25 yards.

West Ham were level after 20 minutes when Dave Dunmore ran 40 yards to score. The Fourth Division side went ahead in the 53rd minute when Rayment scored from a cross from Morton. Eleven minutes later John Bond sent a bad back pass to goalkeeper Rhodes and Robson nipped in to score. On 68 minutes John Dick pulled a goal back but gallant Darlington held on for a famous victory.

1961/62

Round One 11th September 1961.

West Ham United 3 (Crawford 2, Woosnam), Plymouth Argyle 2 (Maloy, Williams). Att: 12,170. Referee: K Burns. West Ham United: Rhodes, Kirkup, Bond, Hurst, Brown, Moore, Scott, Woosnam, Sealey, Dick, Crawford.
Plymouth Argyle: Maclaren, Robertson, Fulton, Williams, Newman, Casey, Anderson, Carter, Kirby, McAnearney, Maloy.

Round Two 9th October 1961.

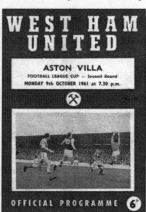

West Ham United 1 (Musgrave), Aston Villa 3 (McParland, Burrows, Bond (og)). Att: 17,775. Referee: G Roper. West Ham United: Leslie, Kirkup, Bond, Hurst, Brown, Moore, Scott, Woosnam, Sealey, Dick, Musgrove.
Aston Villa: Sidebottom, Neal, Aitken, Tindall, Sleeuwenhoek, McMorran, McEwan, Baker, McParland, Wylie, Burrows.

1962/63

Round One 26th September 1962

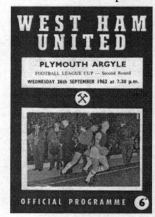

West Ham United 6 (Peters, Byrne 3, Musgrove, Hurst), Plymouth Argyle 0. Att: 9,714. Referee: E Jennings. West Ham United: Leslie, Bond, Burkett, Peters, Brown, Moore, Scott, Boyce, Byrne, Hurst, Musgrove. Plymouth Argyle: Maclaren, Robertson, Fulton, Williams, Wyatt, Newman, Corbett, Jackson, Garden, Thorne, Anderson.

The Hammers were in top form and avenged their FA Cup defeat at Plymouth in the previous season. Martin Peters started the rout after 3 minutes when he headed home following a corner from Tony Scott. Two more headers made the score 3-0; in the 18th minute Geoff Hurst centred to Johnny Byrne to score and on 30 minutes Malcolm Musgrove chipped to Byrne for his second.

Seven minutes before half-time a lob from Scott was handled by Fulton and Byrne completed his hat-trick from the spot. In the 51st minute Musgrove converted Byrnes pass. It was left to Hurst to complete the scoring on 58 minutes. A seventh almost followed when a typical John Bond drive was headed out by Newman.

Round Two 16th October 1962

Rotherham United 3 (Kirkman, Waterhouse, Weston), West Ham United 1 (Hurst).
Att: 11,581. Referee: F Cowan.
Rotherham United: Ironside ,Jackson, Morgan, Lambert, Madden, Waterhouse, Weston, Kirkman, Bennett, Houghton, Taylor.
West Ham United: Leslie, Bond, Burkett, Bovington, Brown, Peters, Scott, Woosnam, Byrne, Hurst, Musgrove.

1963/64

Round Two 25th September 1963.

West Ham United 2 (Scott, Byrne), Leyton Orient 1 (Bolland).
Att: 11,800. Referee: J Cooke
West Ham United: Standen, Kirkup, Burkett, Bovington, Bickles, Moore, Sealey, Boyce, Peters, Byrne, Scott.
Leyton Orient: Davies, Charlton, Lewis, Lucas, Bishop, Lea, Deeley, Mason, Bolland, Ward, Musgrove.

Round Three 16th October 1963.

Aston Villa 0, West Ham United 2 (Bond, Britt).
Att: 11,194. Referee: V O'Callaghan.
Aston Villa: Sims, Wright, Aitken, Crowe, Sleeuwenhoek, Tindall, Baker, Wylie, Hateley, Woosnam, Burrows.
West Ham United: Standen, Bond, Burkett, Peters, Brown, Moore, Sealey, Boyce, Britt, Hurst, Brabrook.

Round Four 4th November 1963

Swindon Town 3 (Rogers, Smith McPherson), West Ham United 3 (Hurst, Brabrook, Boyce).
Att: 12,050. Referee: E Jennings.
Swindon Town: Turner, Dawson, Trollope, Morgan, McPherson, Woodruff, French, Hunt, Smith Summerbee, Rogers.

West Ham United: Standen, Bond, Burkett, Peters, Brown, Charles, Sealey, Boyce, Britt, Hurst, Brabrook.

Round Four replay: 25th November 1963.

West Ham United 4 (Hurst, Brabrook, Byrne, Scott), Swindon Town 1 (Rogers).
Att: 15,778. Referee: J Taylor.
West Ham United: Standen, Bond, Burkett, Charles, Brown, Moore, Scott, Boyce, Byrne, Hurst, Brabrook.
Swindon Town: Turner, Morgan, Trollope, Sproates, Hallett, Woodruff, French, Summerbee, Smith Smart, Rogers.

Second Division Swindon were knocked out of the League Cup by a sparkling display from Johnny Byrne. The England international had a hand in three goals and scored one himself.

In the first minute Geoff Hurst put the Hammers ahead by volleying home a pass from Byrne. The lead was kept until half-time and another quick goal was added in the second half when Byrne headed against the crossbar; Brabrook nodded home the rebound.

On 62 minutes Swindon hit back when Rogers beat Standen with a 20 yard shot. Then in the 67th minute Byrne scored the best goal of the night when he went on a 30 yard run, beating two defenders before hitting a great shot past the keeper. Right-winger Tony Scott completed the scoring in the 84th minute following a pass from Byrne.

Quarter-final 16th December 1963.

West Ham United 6 (Byrne 3, Boyce, Hurst, Scott), Workington 0.
Att: 10,160.
Referee: R Tinkler.
West Ham United: Standen, Bond, Burkett, Bovington, Brown, Moore, Brabrook, Boyce, Byrne, Hurst, Scott.
Workington: Ower, Johnston, Lumsden, Furphy, Brown, Burkinshaw, Middlemass, Timmins, Carr, Moran, Martin.

Fourth Division Workington were brushed aside with ease by the Hammers slick passing and the goalscoring qualities of Johnny Byrne. The England international duo of Byrne and Bobby Moore were the stars of the game.

In the 12th minute a cross from Geoff Hurst was touched home by Byrne. Then the goals flowed as follows;
20 minutes: Ronnie Boyce with a neat shot after a pass from Brabrook
38 minutes: Hurst with a header following a Scott corner
41 minutes: Byrne scoring from another Hurst cross
50 minutes: Scott heading in a cross from Brabrook
52 minutes: Byrne completed his hat-trick slamming home a cross from Scott.

Semi-final, first leg 5th February 1964

Leicester City 4 (Keyworth Roberts, Stringfellow, McLintock), West Ham United 3 (Hurst, 2 Sealey). Att: 14,087. Referee: E Crawford. Leicester City: Banks, Sjoberg, Norman, McLintock, King, Appleton, Hodgson, Roberts, Keyworth Gibson, Stringfellow.
West Ham United: Standen, Bond, Burkett, Peters, Brown, Moore, Sealey, Boyce, Byrne, Hurst, Brabrook.

This amazing soccer spectacle deserved more than the 14,087 fans that came through the Filbert Street turnstiles. The Hammers were losing 3-0 after 20 minutes but made a remarkable recovery.

Keyworth scored for the Foxes after 3 minutes after taking a pass from Gibson. It was the brilliance of Gibson who fashioned goals for Roberts on 13 minutes and for Stringfellow six minutes later.

Geoff Hurst cut the deficit when he hit a smart goal in the 23rd minute. In the second half it was Gibson again who gave a fine pass to McLintock to score a fourth goal after 50 minutes.

Then came a Hammers fightback as first Hurst netted in the 70th minute. Finally, eight minutes from time, Alan Sealey netted from a pass from Moore to set up an exciting second leg clash.

Semi-final, second leg 23rd March 1964.

West Ham United 0, Leicester City 2 (McLintock, Gibson). Att: 27,393. Referee: J Finney. West Ham United: Standen, Bond, Burkett, Bovington, Brown, Moore, Brabrook, Boyce, Byrne, Hurst, Sissons. Leicester City: Banks, Sjoberg, Norman, McLintock, King, Appleton, Hodgson, Cross, Roberts, Gibson, Stringfellow.

All out attack from the Hammers left gaps in the defence, which led to Leicester's first goal in the 33rd minute. With Gordon Banks in good form in the Leicester goal there was no way back for the home team.

1964/65

Round Two 30th September 1964

Sunderland 4 (Mulhall, Mitchinson, Sharkey, Usher), West Ham United 1 (Brabrook).
Att: 22,382. Referee: P Rhodes.
Sunderland: McLaughan, Irwin, Ashurst, Harvey, Hurley, McNab, Usher, Herd, Sharkey, Mitchinson, Mulhall.
West Ham United: Standen, Bond, Burkett, Bovington, Brown, Peters, Brabrook, Boyce, Byrne, Hurst, Sissons.

1965/66

Round Two 21st September 1965

 Bristol, Rovers 3 (Brown, Petts, Jarman), West Ham United 3 (Hurst, 2 Byrne).
Att: 18,354. Referee: E Jennings.
Bristol Rovers: Hall, Hilliard, Jones G, Petts, Stone, Mabbutt, Jarman, Brown, Biggs, Jones R, Munro.
West Ham United: Dickie, Kirkup, Burkett, Bovington, Charles, Moore, Bennett, Peters, Hurst, Byrne, Sissons.

Round Two replay 29th September 1965 West Ham United 3 (Byrne 2, Hurst), Bristol Rovers 2 (Petts, Jones R).

 Att: 13,160. Referee: G Roper.
West Ham United: Dickie, Kirkup, Burkett, Bovington, Brown, Charles, Bennett, Peters, Hurst, Byrne, Sissons.
Bristol Rovers: Hall, Hilliard, Jones G, Petts, Stone, Mabbutt, Jarman, Brown, Biggs, Jones R, Munro.

Round Three 13th October 1965

 West Ham United 4 (Hurst 2, Brabrook, Burnett), Mansfield Town 0.
Att: 11,590. Referee: N Burtenshaw.
West Ham United: Standen, Burnett, Charles, Bovington, Brown, Moore, Brabrook, Peters, Britt, Hurst, Sissons.

Mansfield Town: Treharne, Nelson, Humble, Hall, Gill, Morris, Gregson, Macready, Middleton, Cheesebrough, Scanlon.

Round Four 3rd November 1965

Rotherham United 1 (Galley), West Ham United 2 (Moore, Hurst).
Att: 13,902. Referee: J Pickles.
Rotherham United: Jones, Wilcockson, Clish, Casper, Madden, Tiler, Lyons, Chappell, Galley, Williams, Pring.
West Ham United: Standen, Burnett, Charles, Bovington, Brown, Moore, Brabrook, Peters, Britt, Hurst, Sissons.

Quarter-final 17th November 1965

Grimsby Town 2 (Tees, Green), West Ham United 2 (Charles, Hurst).
Att: 16,281.
Referee: P Rhodes.
Grimsby Town: Wright, Dobson, Taylor, Davidson, Jobling, Clifton, Collins, Tees, Green, Foster, Hill.
West Ham United: Standen, Burnett, Charles, Bovington, Brown, Moore, Brabrook, Peters, Hurst, Britt, Sissons.

Quarter-final replay 15th December 1965

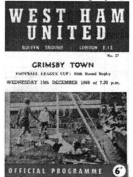

West Ham United 1 (Hurst), Grimsby Town 0.
Att: 17,500 Referee: W Clements.
West Ham United: Standen, Kirkup, Charles, Bovington, Brown, Moore, Brabrook, Peters, Byrne, Hurst, Sissons.
Grimsby Town: Wright, Thompson, Taylor, Davidson, Jobling, Clifton, Collins, Tees, Green, Foster, Hill.

Semi-final, first leg 20th December 1965

West Ham United 5 (Bovington, Byrne, Brabrook, Hurst, Sissons), Cardiff City 2 (Andrews 2).
Att: 19,980. Referee: R Tinkler.
West Ham United: Standen, Kirkup, Charles, Bovington, Brown, Moore, Brabrook, Peters, Byrne, Hurst, Sissons.
Cardiff City: Wilson, Harrington, Rodrigues, Hole, Murray, Houston, Farrell, Harkin, Andrews, Williams, King.

West Ham survived some rough tackling from the Welsh team to take a healthy lead to Wales for the second leg of this semi-final. The Hammers went in front on six minutes when Geoff Hurst lobbed the ball to Eddie Bovington who headed home.

Just after that Jim Standen saved well from King and Andrews hit the West Ham crossbar. Just 3 minutes before the interval Bovington pulled the ball back to Johnny Byrne who swept it into the net. After 66 minutes goalkeeper Wilson dropped a shot from Byrne and Peter Brabrook was on hand to score.

Nine minutes later and John Sissons scored a great goal after running past two defenders.

There was a dramatic ending to the game as the Bluebirds scored two quick goals. First Harkin passed to Andrews who scored. Then two minutes later Andrews was allowed to score his second. In the last minute Hurst completed the scoring as the ball bounced back to him off a defender.

Semi-final, second leg 2nd February 1966

Cardiff City 1 (Johnston), West Ham United 5 (Hurst 2, Peters 2, Burnett). Att: 14,315. Referee: W Clements.
Cardiff City: Davies, Coldrick, Yorath, Hole, Murray, Williams, Lewis, Johnston, Andrews, King, Farrell.
West Ham United: Standen, Burnett, Burkett, Bovington, Brown, Moore, Brabrook, Peters, Britt, Hurst, Sissons.

Final, first leg 9th March 1966

West Ham United 2 (Moore, Byrne), West Bromwich Albion 1 (Astle). Att: 28,323. Referee: D Smith
West Ham United: Standen, Burnett, Burkett, Peters, Brown, Moore, Brabrook, Boyce, Byrne, Hurst, Dear.
West Bromwich Albion: Potter, Cram, Fairfax, Fraser, Campbell, Williams, Brown, Astle, Kaye, Lovett, Clark.

Final, second leg 23rd March 1966

West Bromwich Albion 4 (Kaye, Brown, Clark, Williams), West Ham United 1 (Peters). *West Bromwich Albion won 5-3 on aggregate.* Att: 31,925. Referee: J Mitchell.
West Bromwich Albion: Potter, Cram, Fairfax Fraser, Campbell, Williams, Brown, Astle, Kaye, Hope, Clark.
West Ham United: Standen, Burnett, Peters, Bovington, Brown, Moore, Brabrook, Boyce, Byrne, Hurst, Sissons.

The Hammers were leading 2-1 from the first leg played at Upton Park and 32,000 were inside the Hawthorns on a chilly evening.

From the start the Albion were well on top and after ten minutes Kaye drove home from a measured cross from Cram. Tony Brown netted number two in 19 minutes putting Albion ahead over the two legs. After 28 minutes Clarke grabbed a third when he darted forward to head home after a shot from Kaye was blocked. In the 35th minute the Albion skipper Williams drilled home from 30 yards after Astle had played the ball back to him.

West Ham rallied a little in the second half and scored a consolation goal through Martin Peters after 75 minutes. However the Albion nearly scored a fifth near the end when Kaye hit the crossbar. This was the last final to be played over two legs and with Albion winning 5-3 on aggregate they qualified for European competition for the first time.

1966/67

Round Two 14th September 1966

West Ham United 1 (Hurst), Tottenham Hotspur 0.
Att: 34,000.
Referee: H New.
West Ham United: Standen, Burnett, Charles, Peters, Brown, Moore, Brabrook, Boyce, Bennett, Hurst, Sissons.
Tottenham Hotspur: Jennings, Kinnear, Knowles, Mullery, Beal, Clayton, Robertson, Greaves, Gilzean, Venables, Saul.

Round Three 5th October 1966

Arsenal 1 (Jenkins), West Ham United 3 (Peters, Hurst 2)
Att: 33,647. Referee: G Roper.
Arsenal: Furnell, Simpson, Storey, Woodward, Ure, Boot, Coakley, Jenkins, Walley, Sammels, Armstrong.
West Ham United: Standen, Burnett, Charles, Peters, Brown, Moore, Brabrook, Boyce, Byrne, Hurst, Sissons.

England's World Cup star Geoff Hurst was the hero as his two goals helped to beat London rivals Arsenal. The Hammers took the lead on 26 minutes when Peters ran 25 yards before heading the ball past Furnell. Three minutes later Jenkins smashed an overhead shot into the net for the equaliser. In the second half Hurst took control and on 52 minutes he headed in a cross from Sissons. Three minutes later he hooked the ball home from another Sissons cross. The happy Hammers were now unbeaten in nine games.

Round Four 7th November 1966

West Ham United 7 (Sissons 3, Hurst 3, Peters), Leeds United 0.
Att: 27,474. Referee: E Jennings.
West Ham United: Standen, Bovington, Charles, Peters, Brown, Moore, Brabrook, Boyce, Byrne, Hurst, Sissons.
Leeds United: Harvey, Reaney, Bell, Bremner, Charlton, Hunter, Madeley, Belfitt, Greenhoff, Giles, O'Grady.

After beating London rivals Fulham 6-1 just 48 hours earlier, cock-a-hoop Hammers went one better against Leeds and recorded their biggest-ever win in the Football League Cup.

Leeds goalkeeper Harvey made saves from Johnny Byrne and Ken Brown in the opening minute but he could not prevent the Hammers opening the scoring a minute later when Byrne slipped the ball out to Sissons on the left wing and his cross shot curled into the net.

Thus with 88 minutes still to play Leeds were forced to come forward in this fourth round tie. That suited West Ham fine and the goals came as follows:

24 minutes: Byrne put Brabrook clear and the winger went past Bell before squaring the ball for Sissons to score his second

35 minutes: In a similar move, this time Peters fed Brabrook who again found Sissons. A low shot past Harvey completed his hat-trick to put the Hammers 3-0 ahead.

41 minutes: This time Sissons began the move. His cross was only half cleared and Brabrook found Peters. His header got the ball to Byrne and his first time shot hit Charlton but Hurst was credited with the goal.

59 minutes: Byrne displayed great control before sending Hurst away. The forward then drown home a hard, low shot after rounding a defender.

79 minutes: Peters dribbled past two defenders before sending a superb right foot shot past the disconsolate Harvey.

81 minutes: Goalkeeper Standen punted the ball downfield and Byrne judged Brabrook's header to perfection. The ball came over and Hurst hammered it home.

Quarter-final 7th December 1966

Blackpool 1 (Charnley), West Ham United 3 (Hurst 2, Byrne). Att: 15,831. Referee: K Stokes.
Blackpool: Waiters, Armfield, Hughes, Fisher, James, McPhee, Skirton, Robson, Charnley, Moir, Lee.
West Ham United: Standen, Burnett, Charles, Bovington, Brown, Moore, Boyce, Hurst, Byrne, Peters, Sissons.

Semi-final, first leg 18th January 1967

West Bromwich Albion 4 (Astle 3, Collard), West Ham United 0.
Att: 29,796. Referee: J Cattlin.
West Bromwich Albion: Sheppard, Cram, Williams, Collard, Jones, Fraser, Brown, Astle, Kaye, Hope, Clark.
West Ham United: Standen, Burnett, Burkett, Bovington, Brown, Moore, Brabrook, Peters, Byrne, Hurst, Sissons.

An out-of-form West Ham crumbled in the face of Astle's first-half hat-trick.

Semi-final, second leg 8th February 1967

West Ham United 2 (Byrne, Hurst), West Bromwich Albion 2 (Hope, Clark).
Att: 35,790. Referee: T Dawes.
West Ham United: Standen, Bovington, Burkett, Peters, Brown, Moore, Brabrook, Boyce, Byrne, Hurst, Sissons.
West Bromwich Albion: Sheppard, Cram, Williams, Collard, Jones, Fraser, Foggo, Brown, Kaye, Hope, Clark.

West Ham worked hard in the opening moments to pull pack the deficit from the first leg. With the crowd in good voice, they took the lead in the 13th minute when Byrne tapped in after Hurst's shot had been beaten out by Sheppard. West Brom's equalizer in the 33rd minute killed off the tie, leaving them to face Third Division QPR in the final.

1967/68

Round Two 13th September 1967

Walsall 1 (Jackson), West Ham United 5 (Brabrook, Peters 2, Hurst, Evans (og)).
Att: 17,752. Referee: R Egan.
Walsall: Ball, Gregg, Evans, Simpson, Bennett, Atthey, Middleton (Jackson), Baker, Murray, McMorran, Taylor.
West Ham United: Standen, Charles, Kitchener, Peters, Cushley, Moore, Redknapp, Boyce, Brabrook, Hurst, Sissons.

The scoreline suggests it was an easy stroll for the Hammers. However the Third Division team had more of the play and were frustrated by the heroics of goalkeeper Jim Standen.

It took only a minute for Peter Brabrook to give the Hammers the lead. After 22 minutes Martin Peters glided home a corner from Harry Redknapp. Then, just before half-time, Geoff Hurst hit home a penalty after Evans had brought down Peters.

On 73 minutes Boyce fouled Baker and from the spot Jackson scored to give Walsall some hope. But in the 83rd minute John Charles crossed for Peters to lob Hammers' fourth. Four minutes later the luckless Evans put through his own net following a shot from Sissons.

Round Three 11th October 1967

West Ham United 4 (Hurst 4), Bolton Wanderers 1 (Byrom).
Att: 20,510. Referee: G Roper.
West Ham United: Ferguson, Bonds, Charles, Peters, Cushley, Moore, Redknapp, Boyce, Brabrook, Hurst, Sissons.
Bolton Wanderers: Hopkinson, Hatton, Farrimond, Ritson, Hulme, Greaves, Rimmer, Bromley, Byrom, Hill, Taylor.

Round Four 1st November 1967

Huddersfield Town 2 (Worthington, Cattlin), West Ham United 0.
Att: 17,729. Referee: D Lyden.
Huddersfield Town: Oldfield, Parkin, Cattlin, Nicholson, Ellam, Meagan, Hellawell, Dobson, Worthington, McGill, Hill.
West Ham United: Ferguson, Bonds, Charles, Peters, Cushley, Moore, Burkett, Boyce (Redknapp), Brabrook, Hurst, Dear.

1968/69

Round Two 4th September 1968

West Ham United 7 (Hurst, 3 Peters, Sissons, Brooking, Redknapp), Bolton Wanderers 2 (Wharton, Taylor). Att: 24,937. Referee: R Spittle. West Ham United: Ferguson, Bonds, Charles, Peters, Stephenson, Moore, Redknapp, Boyce, Brooking, Hurst, Sissons.
Bolton Wanderers: Hopkinson, Ritson, Farrimond, Williams, Hulme, Hatton, Wharton, Hill, Greaves, Bromley, Taylor.

Led by hat-trick star Geoff Hurst the Hammers scored seven to crush Second Division Bolton. After 4 minutes Hatton handled and Hurst scored from the resulting penalty. A few minutes later Martin Peters scored with an excellent header following a cross from Harry Redknapp. On 29 minutes Johnny Sissons lobbed to Hurst who, with a scissors kick, scored his second. Three minutes later Hurst completed his hat-trick to demoralise Bolton.

The Trotters got a goal back in the 40th minute when Wharton converted a penalty after Greaves had been brought down. The Hammers strolled through the second half and Sissons scored on 69 minutes before Taylor crashed in a goal for Bolton on 78 minutes. A minute later Sissons set up a goal for Trevor Brooking and Redknapp scored with a low drive in the final minute.

Round Three 25th September 1968

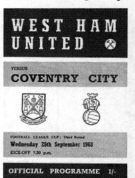

West Ham United 0, Coventry City 0. Att: 27,594. Referee: R Johnson. West Ham United: Ferguson, Bonds, Charles, Peters, Stephenson, Moore, Redknapp, Boyce, Brooking, Hurst, Sissons. Coventry City: Glazier, Coop, Cattlin, Curtis, Setters, Hill, Hannigan, Machin, Hunt, Carr, Clements.

Round Three replay 1st October 1968

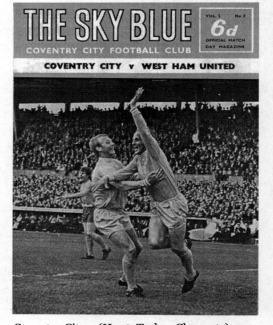

Coventry City 3 (Hunt, Tudor, Clements), West Ham United 2 (Hurst, Peters). Att: 25,988. Referee: I Jones. Coventry City: Glazier, Coop, Bruck, Machin, Curtis, Hill, Hunt, Carr, Tudor, Gibson (Hannigan), Clements. West Ham United: Ferguson, Howe, Charles, Peters, Cushley, Moore, Redknapp, Boyce, Brooking, Hurst, Dear.

1969/70

Round Two 3rd September 1969

West Ham United 4 (Lampard, Best, Hurst 2), Halifax Town 2 (Lawther, Wallace).
Att: 20,717. Referee: J Osborne.
West Ham United: Ferguson, Bonds, Lampard, Peters, Stephenson, Moore, Redknapp, Lindsay, Brooking, Hurst, Best.
Halifax Town: Smith Burgin, Pickering, Lennard, McCarthy, Robertson, Shawcross, Hill, Ryden (Wallace), Flower.

In an untidy match it was left to Geoff Hurst to brighten the evening with two well-taken goals. After 15 minutes a Frank Lampard free-kick opened the scoring for the Hammers. On 34 minutes a drive from Bobby Moore was diverted into the net by Clyde Best. The Third Division team were back in the game just after half-time when Lawther scored a simple goal. Then came the Hurst double, the first being a great header from Redknapp's cross. In the last minute Wallace scored for the Yorkshire side to give them a more respectable scoreline.

Round Three 3rd, September 1969

Nottingham Forest 1 (Lyons), West Ham United 0.
Att: 20,939. Referee: N Burtenshaw.
Nottingham Forest: Hill, Hindley, Winfield, Chapman, Hennessey, Newton, Rees, Lyons, Hilley, Barnwell, Moore.
West Ham United: Ferguson, Bonds, Lampard, Boyce, Stephenson, Moore, Redknapp, Brooking, Hurst, Cross, Peters.

1970/71

Round Two 9th September 1970

West Ham United 1 (Eustace), Hull City-0.
Att: 19,116. Referee: N Burtenshaw.
West Ham United: Grotier, Bonds, Lampard, Eustace, Stephenson, Moore, Best, Redknapp, Hurst, Greaves, Howe.
Hull City: McKechnie, Beardsley, De Vries, Wilkinson, Neill, Simpkin, Lord, Houghton (Greenwood), Chilton, Wagstaff, Jarvis.

Round Three 6th October 1970

Coventry City 3 (Martin, O'Rourke, Carr), West Ham United 1 (Hurst).
Att: 19,362. Referee: A Jones.
Coventry City: Glazier, Coop, Bruck, Clements, Blockley, Strong, Hunt, Carr, Martin, O'Rourke, Alderson.
West Ham United: Grotier, Bonds, Lampard, Lindsay, Stephenson, Moore, Ayris, Best, Hurst, Brooking, Eustace.

1971/72

Round Two 8th September 1971

West Ham United 1 (Bonds), Cardiff City 1 (Foggon).
Att: 24,432. Referee: J Taylor.
West Ham United: Ferguson, McDowell, Lampard, Bonds, Taylor, Moore, Ayris, Best, Hurst, Brooking, Robson.
Cardiff City: Eadie, Jones (Parsons), Bell, Sutton, Murray, Phillips, Gibson, Clark, Woodruff, Warboys, Foggon.

Round Two replay 22nd, September 1971

Cardiff City 1 (Clark), West Ham United 2 (Hurst 2).
Att: 30,100. Referee: J Taylor.
Cardiff City: Eadie, Jones, Bell, Sutton, Murray, Phillips, Gibson, Clark, Woodruff, Warboys, Hoy.
West Ham United: Ferguson, McDowell, Lampard, Bonds, Taylor, Moore, Redknapp, Best, Hurst, Brooking, Robson.

Round Three 6th October 1971

West Ham United 0, Leeds United 0.
Att: 35,890. Referee: R Matthewson.
West Ham United: Ferguson, McDowell, Lampard, Bonds, Taylor, Moore, Redknapp, Best, Hurst, Brooking, Robson.
Leeds United: Sprake, Davie, Cooper, Bremner, Charlton, Hunter, Lorimer, Yorath Belfitt, Giles, Madeley.

Round Three replay 20th October 1971

Leeds United 0, West Ham United 1 (Best).
Att: 26,504. Referee: R Matthewson.
Leeds United: Harvey, Reaney, Cooper, Bremner, Charlton, Hunter, Lorimer, Clarke, Jones (Gray), Giles, Madeley.
West Ham United: Ferguson, McDowell, Lampard, Bonds, Taylor, Moore, Redknapp, Best, Hurst, Brooking, Robson.

Round Four 27th October 1971

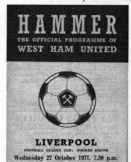

West Ham United 2 (Hurst, Robson), Liverpool 1 (Graham).
Att: 40,878. Referee: D Turner.
West Ham United: Ferguson, McDowell, Lampard, Bonds, Taylor, Moore, Redknapp, Best, Hurst (Howe), Brooking, Robson.
Liverpool: Clemence, Lawler, Ross, Smith Lloyd, Hughes, Graham, Evans, Heighway, Toshack, Callaghan.

Quarter-final 17th November 1971

West Ham United 5 (Robson 3, Best 2), Sheffield United 0. Att: 36,834. Referee: D Smith. West Ham United: Ferguson, McDowell, Lampard, Bonds, Taylor, Moore, Redknapp, Best, Hurst (Howe), Brooking, Robson. Sheffield United: Hope, Badger, Goulding, Flynn, Colquhoun, Hockey, Woodward, Salmons, Reece, Currie, Scullion.

The Hammers marched into the League Cup semi-finals with a scintillating display of attacking football. Leading the plaudits was striker Pop Robson who claimed a hat-trick.

West Ham began with a flourish as Robson headed home after only five minutes. After 32 minutes he scored again following a pass from Hurst. Seven minutes later the majestic Clyde Best curled in a shot to make it 3-0. On 76 minutes Best hit a 30-yarder which goalkeeper Hope half held but then dropped into the net. The rout was complete when Robson scored his third goal four minutes from time.

Semi-final first leg 8th December 1971

Stoke City 1 (Dobing), West Ham United 2 (Hurst, Best). Att: 36,400. Referee: A Morrissey. Stoke City: Banks, Marsh, Pejic, Bernard, Bloor, Jump, Conroy, Greenhoff, Ritchie, Dobing, Eastham. West Ham United: Ferguson, McDowell, Lampard, Bonds, Taylor, Moore, Redknapp, Best, Hurst, Brooking, Robson.

Semi-final second leg 15th December 1971

West Ham United 0, Stoke City 1 (Ritchie). Att: 38,771. Referee: K Walker. West Ham United: Ferguson, McDowell, Lampard, Bonds, Taylor, Moore, Redknapp, Best, Hurst, Brooking, Robson. Stoke City: Banks, Marsh, Pejic, Bernard, Bloor, Skeels, Conroy, Greenhoff, Ritchie, Dobing, Eastham (Mahoney).

Semi-final replay at Hillsborough 5th January 1972

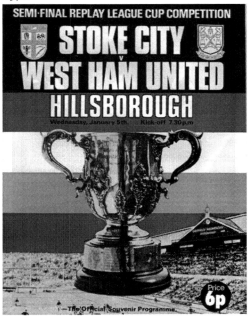

Stoke City 0, West Ham United 0 Att: 46,196. Referee: R Matthewson. Stoke City: Banks, Marsh, Pejic, Bernard, Smith Bloor, Conroy, Dobing, Ritchie, Greenhoff (Skeels), Eastham. West Ham United: Ferguson, McDowell, Lampard, Bonds, Taylor, Moore, Redknapp, Best, Hurst, Brooking, Robson.

Semi-final second replay at Old Trafford 26th January 1972

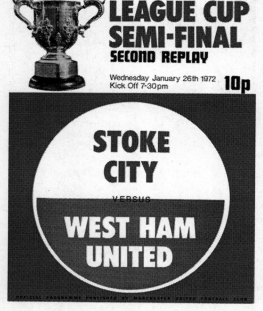

LEAGUE CUP SEMI-FINAL SECOND REPLAY

Wednesday January 26th 1972
Kick Off 7-30pm 10p

STOKE CITY

VERSUS

WEST HAM UNITED

OFFICIAL PROGRAMME PUBLISHED BY MANCHESTER UNITED FOOTBALL CLUB

Stoke City 3 (Bernard, Dobing, Conroy), West Ham United 2 (Bonds, Brooking).
Att: 49,247. Referee: P Partridge.
Stoke City: Banks, Marsh, Pejic, Bernard, Smith Bloor, Conroy, Greenhoff, Ritchie, Dobing, Eastham.
West Ham United: Ferguson, McDowell, Lampard, Bonds, Taylor, Moore, Redknapp (Eustace), Best, Hurst, Brooking, Robson.

For twists, turns, upheavals and sheer football drama this was one of the best League Cup ties that has ever been played. After home and away meetings and a 0-0 draw at Sheffield this semi-final was now to be settled at Old Trafford.

In the 13th minute Stoke's Conroy chased a ball towards the West Ham goal and caught goalkeeper Bobby Ferguson on the side of the head. Ferguson was badly dazed and was in no state to continue. Captain Bobby Moore took over the green jersey and soon after had to face a penalty conceded by John McDowell as he tried to rectify a bad back pass. Stoke defender Bernard took the kick and Moore dived to his right to parry the shot. Unfortunately it rebounded to Bernard who then scored. The ten men rallied and first Billy Bonds equalised after a strong shot. Soon after Bonds helped create a goal which Brooking scored with a fine volley.

Ferguson came out for the second half, so the Hammers were back to full strength. Early in the half Dobing stole in to equalise and Stoke were now on top. Conroy put in a shot from beyond the area which sailed into the net past a still-dazed Ferguson. West Ham rallied but their earlier efforts when down to 10-men left them with nothing in reserve.

Goalkeeper Ferguson said afterwards that he could not remember anything about the match. It was a marvellous game that will live forever in the memory of those who attended.

1972/73

Round Two 6th September 1972

West Ham United 2 (McDowell, Best), Bristol City 1 (Galley).
Att: 17,688.
Referee: N Paget.
West Ham United: Grotier, McDowell, Lampard, Bonds, Taylor, Moore, Tyler, Best, Holland, Brooking, Robson.
Bristol City: Cashley, Wilson, Drysdale, Sweeney, Rodgers (Broomfield), Merrick, Tainton, Spring, Galley, Gow, Ritchie.

Round Three 4th October 1972

Stockport County 2 (Russell, Spratt), West Ham United 1 (Best).
Att: 13,410. Referee: P Partridge
Stockport County: Ogley, Ingle, Charter, Spratt, Hart, Ashworth, Garbett, Ryden, Griffiths, Russell, Davidson.
West Ham United: Grotier, McDowell, Lampard, Bonds, Taylor, Moore, Tyler, Best, Holland, Brooking, Robson.

1973/74

Round Two 8th October 1973

West Ham United 2 (MacDougall, Robson), Liverpool 2 (Cormack, Heighway).
Att: 25,840.
Referee: J Taylor
West Ham United: Day, McDowell, Lampard, Coleman, Taylor, Lock (Holland), Ayris, Best, MacDougall, Brooking, Robson.
Liverpool: Clemence, Lawler, Lindsay, Smith, Lloyd, Hughes, Keegan, Cormack, Heighway, Hall, Callaghan.

Round Two replay 29th October 1973

Liverpool 1 (Toshack), West Ham United 0.
Att: 26,002.
Referee: J Taylor.
Liverpool: Clemence, Lawler, Lindsay, Smith, Lloyd, Hughes, Keegan, Cormack, Heighway, Toshack, Callaghan.
West Ham United: Day, Coleman, Lampard, Bonds, Taylor, Moore, Tyler, McDowell, Best, Brooking, Lock (Holland).

1974/75

Round Two 11th September 1974

Tranmere Rovers 0 West Ham United 0.
Att: 8,638. Referee: A Grey.
Tranmere Rovers: Johnson, Matthias, Flood, Moore, Philpotts, Veitch, Coppell, Palios, Young, Tynan, Crossley.
West Ham United: Day, McDowell, Lampard, Bonds, Taylor, Lock, Ayris, Paddon, Holland, Brooking, Best.

Round Two replay 18th September 1974

West Ham United 6 (Bonds, 2, Gould, 3, Ayris), Tranmere Rovers 0.
Att: 15,854. Referee: A Grey.
West Ham United: Day, McDowell, Lampard, Bonds, Taylor, Lock, Ayris, Paddon, Gould, Brooking, Robson.
Tranmere Rovers: Johnson, Matthias, Flood, Moore, Philpotts, Veitch, Coppell, Palios (Webb), Mitchell, Tynan, Crossley.

Round Three 8th October 1974

Fulham 2 (Mullery, Slough), West Ham United 1 (Brooking).
Att: 29,611. Referee: H New.
Fulham: Mellor, Cutbush, Strong, Mullery, Lacy, Moore, Conway, Slough, Busby, Lloyd, Barrett.
West Ham United: Day, Coleman, Lampard, Bonds, Taylor, Lock, Ayris (Holland), Paddon, Gould, Brooking, Robson.

The attendance of 29,611 was the biggest crowd seen at Craven Cottage for 4 years. No doubt many had come to see Bobby Moore playing against his former club for the first time. The Hammers prompted by Billy Bonds were on top in the early stages.

On 34 minutes a cross from Paddon found Trevor Brooking who struck a superb volley to put the East London side ahead. The second half began with a Fulham equaliser. Moore tapped a free kick to Mullery who drove it past Mervyn Day.

After 53 minutes the floodlights failed and the teams were led back into the dressing rooms. There was a 30-minute hold up before the teams returned, albeit to dimmed lights. On 59 minutes Slough hit the Fulham winner when he curled a shot past Day.

The clubs were to meet again the following May in the FA Cup Final with the Hammers winning on that occasion.

1975/76

Round Two 8th September 1975

West Ham United 0, Bristol City 0.
Att: 19,837. Referee: A Robinson.
West Ham United: Day, McDowell, Lampard, Bonds, Taylor, Lock, Holland (Ayris), Paddon, Jennings, Brooking, Robson.
Bristol City: Cashley, Sweeney, Drysdale, Gow, Collier, Merrick, Tainton, Ritchie, Mann, Cheeseley, Brolly (Gillies).

Round Two replay 24th September 1975

Bristol City 1 (Cheeseley), West Ham United 3 (Brooking, Best, Taylor A).
Att: 19,643. Referee: A Robinson
Bristol City: Cashley, Sweeney, Drysdale, Gow, Collier, Merrick, Tainton, Ritchie, Mann, Cheeseley, Brolly (Gillies).
West Ham United Day, McDowell, Lampard, Bonds, Taylor T, Lock, Taylor A, Paddon, Best, Brooking, Holland.

Round Three 8th October 1975

West Ham United 3 (Paddon, Robson, Bonds), Darlington 0.
Att: 19,844. Referee: R Kirkpatrick.
West Ham United: Day, McDowell, Lampard, Bonds, Taylor T, Lock (Jennings), Robson, Paddon, Best, Taylor A, Holland.
Darlington: Ogley, Nattrass, Cochrane, Cattrell, Noble, Blant, Holbrook (Rowles), Sinclair, Webb, Crosson, Young.

Round Four 12th November 1975

Tottenham Hotspur 0, West Ham United 0.
Att: 49,125. Referee: M Sinclair.
Tottenham Hotspur: Jennings, Naylor, McAlister, Pratt, Young, Osgood, Coates. Perryman, Duncan (Conn), Jones, Neighbour
West Ham United: Day, McDowell, Lock, Bonds, Taylor T, Coleman, Taylor A, Paddon, Holland, Brooking, Robson.

Round Four replay 24th November 1975

West Ham United 0, Tottenham Hotspur 2 (Duncan, Young).
Att: 38,443. Referee: M Sinclair.
West Ham United: Day, McDowell, Lampard, Bonds, Taylor T, Lock, Taylor A, Paddon, Holland, Brooking (Jennings), Robson.
Tottenham Hotspur: Jennings, Naylor, McAlister, Pratt, Young, Osgood, Coates, Perryman, Duncan, Jones, Neighbour.

1976/77

Round Two 1st September 1976

West Ham United 3, (Holland 2, Paddon) Barnsley 0.
Att: 17,889. Referee: R Lewis.
West Ham United: Day, Coleman, McGiven, Holland, Green, Bonds, Taylor T, Paddon, Taylor A, Brooking, Jennings.
Barnsley: Springett, Murphy, Gorry, Otulakowski, Burke, Pickering, Felton, Peachey, Joicey, Brown, Millar (Price).

Round Three 21st September 1976

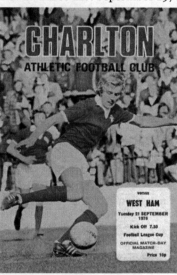

Charlton Athletic 0, West Ham United 1 (Taylor A).
Att: 32,898. Referee: J Homewood.
Charlton Athletic: Wood, Berry, Warman, Hunt, Giles, Curtis, Powell, Hales, Flanagan, Bowman, Peacock.
West Ham United: Day, Coleman, McGiven, Bonds, Green, Taylor T, Jennings, Paddon, Taylor A, Brooking, Lock.

Round Four 27th October 1976

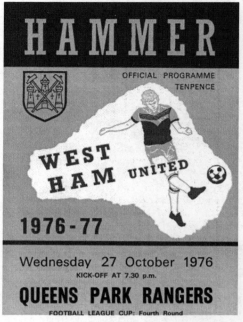

West Ham United 0, Queen's Park Rangers 2 (Bowles, Clement).
Att: 24,565. Referee: R Capey.
West Ham United: Day, Bonds, Lampard, Curbishley, Lock, Taylor T, Orhan, Paddon, Devonshire, Brooking, Robson.
Queen's Park Rangers: Parkes, Clement, Gillard, Hollins, McLintock, Webb, Thomas (Leach), Kelly, Masson, Bowles, Givens.

1977/78

Round Two 30th August 1977

Nottingham Forest 5 (Bowyer, 2, Woodcock, Withe, O'Neill), West Ham United 0.
Att: 18,224. Referee: D, Turner.
Nottingham Forest: Middleton, Anderson, Clark, McGovern, Lloyd, Burns, O'Neill, Bowyer, Withe, Woodcock, Robertson.
West Ham United: Day, Lampard, Brush, Pike, Green, Lock, Taylor A, Robson, Radford, Curbishley, Devonshire.

1978/79

Round Two 30th August 1978

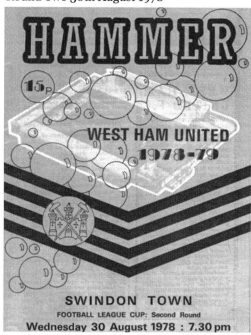

West Ham United 1 (Robson), Swindon Town 2 (Miller, Guthrie).
Att: 19,672. Referee: M Taylor.
West Ham United: Ferguson, Lampard, Brush, Holland, Taylor T, Bonds, Curbishley, Devonshire, Cross, Taylor A (Pike), Robson B.
Swindon Town: Ogden, McLaughlin, Ford, McHale, Aizlewood, Stroud, Miller, Carter, Guthrie (Kamara), Bates, Williams.

1979/80

Round Two first leg 28th August 1979
West Ham United 3 (Brooking, Pearson, Cross), Barnsley 1 (Glavin).
Att: 12,320. Referee: J Burden
West Ham United: Parkes, Lampard, Brush, Bonds, Martin, Holland, Pike, Pearson, Cross, Brooking, Devonshire.
Barnsley: Pierce, Flavell, Collins, Glavin, Dugdale, McCarthy, Little, Riley, Pugh, Millar, Bell.

Round Two second leg 4th September 1979
Barnsley 0, West Ham United 2 (Cross 2).
Att: 15,898. Referee: K Walmsley.
Barnsley: Pierce, Flavell (Millar), Collins, Glavin, Dugdale, McCarthy, Little, Riley, Pugh, Banks, Bell.
West Ham United: Parkes, Lampard, Brush, Bonds, Stewart, Holland, Pike, Banton, Cross, Brooking, Morgan.

Round Three 25th September 1979

West Ham United 1 (Cross), Southend United 1 (Pountney).
Att: 19,658. Referee: R Lewis.
West Ham United: Parkes, Stewart, Brush, Bonds, Martin, Holland, Allen, Lansdowne, Cross, Brooking, Devonshire.
Southend United: Cawston, Dudley, Moody, Cusack, Yates, Stead, Otulakowski, Pountney, Morris, Tuohy, Gray.

Round Three replay 1st October 1979

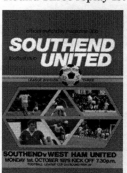

Southend United 0, West Ham United 0.
Att: 22,497. Referee: J Sewell.
Southend United: Cawston, Dudley, Moody, Cusack, Yates (Walker), Stead, Otulakowski, Pountney, Morris, Tuohy, Gray.
West Ham United: Parkes, Stewart, Brush, Bonds, Martin, Holland, Allen, Lansdowne, Cross, Brooking, Devonshire.

Round Three second replay 8th October 1979

West Ham United 5 (Lansdowne 3, Holland, Stewart), Southend United 1 (Gray).
Att: 19,718. Referee: M Baker.
West Ham United: Parkes, Stewart, Smith, Bonds, Martin, Holland, Allen, Lansdowne, Cross, Brooking, Pike.
Southend United: Cawston, Dudley, Moody, Cusack, Walker, Stead, Otulakowski (Hull), Morris, Pountney, Hadley, Gray.

After two drawn games this tie finally got a winner. Smiling at the end was West Ham's 20-year old Billy Lansdowne clutching the match ball after his fine hat-trick.

It was the Shrimpers who took the lead in the 22nd minute when Morris crossed for Gray to head home. Three minutes later Lansdowne was on hand to score after David Cross had headed against the bar. Six minutes later the young striker scored again following a cross from Pat Holland.

A minute into the second half Lansdowne completed his hat-trick. The fourth goal followed on the hour when Holland finished a move from Brooking. Then with 10 minutes remaining Ray Stewart scored from the penalty spot after Paul Allen had been brought down by Dudley.

Round Four 31st October 1979

Sunderland 1 (Brown), West Ham United 1 (Pike). Att: 30,302. Referee: G Nolan
Sunderland: Siddall, Whitworth, Gilbert, Clarke, Hindmarch, Elliott, Arnott, Lee, Brown, Robson, Powell.
West Ham United: Parkes, Stewart, Lampard, Bonds, Martin, Holland, Allen, Pike, Cross, Brooking (Lansdowne), Devonshire.

Round Four replay 5th November 1979

West Ham United 2 (Martin, Cross), Sunderland 1 (Brown). Att: 24,454. Referee: S Bates.
West Ham United: Ferguson, Stewart, Lampard, Bonds, Martin, Holland, Allen, Pike, Cross, Devonshire, Lansdowne.
Sunderland: Siddall, Whitworth, Bolton, Clarke, Elliott, Hindmarch, Arnott, Gilbert, Brown, Rowell, Dunn.

Quarter-final 4th December 1979

West Ham United 0, Nottingham Forest 0. Att: 35,856. Referee: A Grey.
West Ham United: Parkes, Stewart, Lampard, Bonds, Martin, Holland, Allen, Pearson, Cross, Brooking, Devonshire. Nottingham Forest: Shilton, Anderson, Gray, Bowyer, Lloyd, Burns, O'Neill, O'Hare, Birtles, Francis, Robertson.

Quarter-final replay 12th December 1979

Nottingham Forest 3 (O'Hare, Birtles, O'Neill), West Ham United 0. Att: 25,462. Referee: N Ashley.
Nottingham Forest: Shilton, Anderson, Gray, Bowyer, Lloyd, Burns, O'Neill, O'Hare, Birtles, Francis, Robertson.
West Ham United: Parkes, Stewart, Lampard, Bonds, Martin, Pike, Allen, Pearson, Cross, Brooking, Devonshire.

1980/81

Round Two first leg 26th August 1980

Burnley 0, West Ham United 2 (Goddard, Cross). Att: 6,818. Referee: D Shaw.
Burnley: Stevenson, Wood, Thomson, Rodaway, Laws, Scott, Dobson, Cassidy, Cavener, Hamilton, Taylor.
West Ham United: Parkes, Stewart, Lampard, Bonds, Martin, Devonshire, Holland, Goddard, Cross, Brooking, Pike.

Round Two second leg 2nd September 1980

West Ham United 4 (Stewart, Goddard, Wood (og), Pike), Burnley 0.
Att: 15,216. Referee: A Seville.
West Ham United: Parkes, Stewart, Lampard, Bonds, Martin, Devonshire, Holland (Allen), Goddard, Cross, Brooking, Pike.
Burnley: Stevenson, Laws, Holt, Scott (Wood), Dobson, Overson, Cassidy, Young, Hamilton, Taylor, Cavener.

Round Three 23rd September 1980

Charlton Athletic 1 (Robinson), West Ham United 2 (Cross 2).
Att: 17,884. Referee: M Taylor.
Charlton Athletic: Wood, Gritt, Warman, Shaw, Berry, Tydeman, Powell, Walsh, Hales, Smith, Robinson.
West Ham United: Parkes, Stewart, Lampard, Bonds, Martin, Devonshire, Barnes, Goddard, Cross, Brush, Pike.

Round Four 28th October 1980

West Ham United 2 (Martin, Cross), Barnsley 1 (Evans). Att: 21,548. Referee: A Glasson.
West Ham United: Parkes, Stewart, Lampard (Allen), Brush, Martin, Devonshire, Holland, Goddard, Cross, Neighbour, Pike.
Barnsley: New, Joyce, Chambers, Glavin, Banks, McCarthy, Evans, Riley, Aylott, Lester, Downes.

Quarter-final 2nd, December 1980

West Ham United 1 (Cross), Tottenham Hotspur 0.
Att: 36,003. Referee: J Hunting.
West Ham United: Parkes, Stewart, Lampard, Bonds, Martin, Devonshire, Holland, Goddard, Cross, Neighbour, Pike.
Tottenham Hotspur: Daines, McAlister, Hughton, Yorath, Lacy, Perryman, Ardiles, Archibald, Villa, Hoddle, Crooks.

Semi-final first leg 27th January 1981

Coventry City 3 (Thompson, 2, Daly), West Ham United 2 (Bonds, Thompson (og)). Att: 35,468. Referee: G Courtney.
Coventry City: Sealey, Thomas, Roberts, Blair, Dyson, Gillespie, Bodak, Daly (Jacobs), Thompson, Hateley, Hunt.

West Ham United: Parkes, Stewart, Brush, Bonds, Martin, Devonshire, Allen, Goddard, Cross, Brooking, Pike.

Semi-final second leg 10th February 1981,

West Ham United 2 (Goddard, Neighbour), Coventry City 0. Att: 36,551. Referee: K Hackett.
West Ham United: Parkes, Stewart, Lampard, Bonds, Martin, Devonshire, Neighbour, Goddard, Cross, Brooking, Pike.
Coventry City: Sealey, Thomas, Roberts, Blair, Dyson, Gillespie, Bodak (Jacobs), Daly, Thompson, Hateley, Hunt.

Final at Wembley Stadium 14th March 1981

Liverpool 1 (Kennedy), West Ham United 1 (Stewart).
Att: 100,000.
Referee: C Thomas.
Liverpool: Clemence, Neal, Kennedy A, Irwin, Kennedy R, Hansen, Dalglish, Lee, Heighway (Case), McDermott, Souness.
West Ham United: Parkes, Stewart, Lampard, Bonds, Martin, Devonshire, Neighbour, Goddard (Pearson), Cross, Brooking, Pike.

The League Cup Final at Wembley was a game of ploy and counter ploy by both sides with little excitement. In the 10th minute Sammy Lee scored for Liverpool but his team-mate Irwin was rightly flagged for off side. Neither side could prise out real openings in a dour struggle and the game moved into extra time.

The pattern did not change in extra time until the last three minutes as the game boiled over into a most exciting finish. A Liverpool free kick on the edge of the area was not

properly cleared which allowed Kennedy to lash home a right foot shot. As Kennedy connected, a linesman flagged as the Hammers defence came out to leave Lee lying well off side. Despite furious protests referee Clive Thomas gave the goal.

With only seconds remaining Devonshire was up-ended dribbling through. Ray Stewart took the free kick and his cannon ball shot was turned aside by Clemence for a corner. From the corner Alvin Martin climbed high to direct a header past Clemence but team mate Terry McDermott could only fling up his fist and turned the header over to concede a penalty. All now depended on Hammers penalty expert Ray Stewart. All the pressure was on him but the ice cool Scot calmly blasted his shot past a despairing Clemence to equalise; then came the final whistle. As the teams left the field West Ham manager John Lyall was booked as he argued with the referee about the Liverpool goal.

Final replay at Villa Park 1st April 1981

Liverpool 2 (Dalglish, Hansen), West Ham United 1 (Goddard).
Att: 36,693. Referee: C Thomas.
Liverpool: Clemence, Neal, Kennedy A, Thompson, Kennedy, R, Hansen, Dalglish, Lee, Rush, McDermott, Case.
West Ham United: Parkes, Stewart, Lampard, Bonds, Martin, Devonshire, Neighbour, Goddard, Cross, Brooking, Pike (Pearson).

The Hammers made a great start to the replay when Jimmy Neighbour went past Alan Hansen and crossed for Paul Goddard to score with a header. Dalglish equalized with a spectacular volley. West Ham fought a strong rearguard action against in-form Liverpool but lost to a Hansen goal that deflected off the knee of Billy Bonds.

1981/82

Round Two first leg 7th October 1981

Derby County 2 (Stewart (og), Hector), West
Ham United 3 (Cross, Brooking, Stewart).
Att: 13,764. Referee: R Bridges.
Derby County: Cherry, Coop, Buckley, Powell
S, Ramage, Osgood (Clayton), Skivington,
Powell B, Hector, Swindlehurst, Emson.
West Ham United: McAlister, Stewart,
Lampard, Bonds, Martin, Devonshire,
Neighbour, Goddard, Cross, Brooking, Pike.

*The Rams were handed a gift goal in the 9th
minute when Ray Stewart attempted to clear
only to put the ball beyond goalkeeper Tom
McAlister. The equaliser came after 29
minutes when David Cross back headed a
cross from Geoff Pike.*

*A minute after the break Derby went
back into the lead when Hector netted his
200th goal for the club. Within two minutes
the Hammers were level again as Cross
slipped a perfect pass to Trevor Brooking
who struck a drive beyond Cherry. Eight
minutes from the end Cross put in a powerful
header which was handled on the line by
defender Ramage. After his earlier blunder
Ray Stewart was pleased to make amends by
blasting home the penalty kick for the
winning goal.*

Round Two second leg 27th October 1981

West Ham United 2
(Goddard 2), Derby
County 0.
Att: 21.043.
Referee: M Taylor.
West Ham United:
Parkes, Stewart,
Lampard, Bonds,
Martin, Devonshire,
Neighbour,
Goddard, Cross,
Brooking, Pike.
Derby County:
Jones, Coop,
Buckley, Powell S, Sheridan, Powell B, Hector
(Gibson), Reid, Clayton, Swindlehurst,
Emson.

Round Three 10th November 1981

West Ham United 2
(Stewart, Cross),
West Bromwich
Albion 2 (Regis,
King).
Att: 24,168. Referee:
T Spencer.
West Ham United:
Parkes, Brush,
Lampard, Stewart,
Martin, Devonshire,
Neighbour, Goddard,
Cross, Brooking,
Pike.
West Bromwich Albion: Grew, Arthur,
Statham, King, Wile, Robertson, Jol, Brown,
Regis, Owen, Mackenzie.

Round Three replay 24th November 1981

West Bromwich Albion 1 (Regis), West Ham United 1 (Stewart).
Att: 15,869. Referee: H King West Bromwich Albion: Grew, Batson, Statham, King, Wile, Robertson, Jol, Brown, Regis, Owen, Mackenzie.
West Ham United: Parkes, Stewart, Lampard, Bonds, Martin, Devonshire, Neighbour, Goddard (Allen), Cross, Brooking, Pike.

Round Three second replay 1st December 1981

West Ham United 0, West Bromwich Albion 1 (Regis).
Att: 24,760.
Referee: B Martin.
West Ham United: Parkes, Stewart, Lampard, Bonds, Martin, Devonshire, Neighbour, Goddard, Cross (Allen), Brooking, Pike.
West Bromwich Albion: Grew, Batson, Statham, King, Wile, Robertson, Jol, Brown, Regis, Owen, Mackenzie.

1982/83

Round Two first leg 6th October 1982

Stoke City 1 (Thomas), West Ham United 1 (Stewart).
Att: 18,079. Referee: H King.
Stoke City: Fox, Parkin, Hampton, Bracewell, Watson, Berry, Maguire, McIlroy, O'Callaghan, Thomas, Chamberlain (Griffiths).
West Ham United: Parkes, Stewart, Lampard, Orr, Martin, Devonshire, Neighbour, Goddard, Clark, Allen, Pike.

Round Two second leg 26th October 1982

West Ham United 2 (Goddard, Clark), Stoke City 1 (Watson).
Att:18,270. Referee: J Martin.
West Ham United: Parkes, Stewart, Lampard, Bonds, Martin, Devonshire, Van der Elst, Goddard, Clark, Allen, Pike (Neighbour).
Stoke City: Harrison, Parkin, Hampton, Bracewell, Watson, McAughtrie, Maguire, McIlroy, O'Callaghan, Thomas, Chamberlain.

Round Three 10th November 1982

Lincoln City 1 (Bell), West Ham United 1 (Goddard).
Att: 13,899. Referee: K Baker.
Lincoln City: Felgate, Carr, Neale, Cockerill, Peake, Thompson, Burke, Turner, Hobson, Bell, Shipley.
West Ham United: Parkes, Stewart, Brush, Bonds, Martin, Devonshire, Orr (Van der Elst), Goddard, Clark, Allen, Pike.

Round Three replay 29th November 1982

West Ham United 2 (Stewart, Clark), Lincoln City 1 (Clark (og)).
Att: 13,686. Referee: A Glasson.
West Ham United: Parkes, Stewart, Lampard, Bonds, Martin, Neighbour (Barnes), Van der Elst, Goddard, Clark, Allen, Pike.
Lincoln City: Felgate, Carr, Neale, Cockerill, Peake, Thompson, Hibberd, Turner, Hobson, Bell, Shipley.

Round Four 7th December 1982

Notts County 3 (McCulloch, Christie, Hunt), West Ham United 3 (Van der Elst 3).
Att: 7,525. Referee: G Tyson.
Notts County: Avramovic, Benjamin, Worthington, Hunt, Kilcline, Richards, Chiedozie, Christie, McCulloch, Hooks, Mair.
West Ham United: Parkes, Stewart, Lampard, Orr, Martin, Devonshire, Van der Elst, Goddard, Clark (Brush), Allen, Pike.

After a dull first half the Meadow Lane faithful were treated to a real thriller in the second period. On 50 minutes a drive from Chiedozie came back to McCulloch who netted. Three minutes later Alvin Martin pulled down Christie and the same player scored from the spot. The Hammers were in trouble but in an amazing comeback led by Van der Elst they got back in the game.

In the 66th minute Devonshire's cross came to Van der Elst who nudged the ball past Avramovic. On 74 minutes Paul Allen hit the post and from the rebound Van der Elst turned the ball in for the equaliser. Five minutes from time to cap a brilliant display Van der Elst stabbed the ball home to complete his hat-trick. The Hammers

however could not hold on to their lead as two minutes later Hunt scrambled in the equaliser.

Round Four replay 21st December 1982

West Ham United 3 (Stewart, Clark, Allen), Notts County 0.
Att: 13.140. Referee: L Shapter.
West Ham United: Parkes, Stewart, Brush, Orr, Martin, Devonshire, Van der Elst, Goddard, Clark, Allen, Pike.
Notts County: Avramovic, Benjamin, Worthington, Hunt, Kilcline, Richards, Chiedozie, Christie, Fashanu, Goodwin, Clarke (Mair).

Quarter-final 18th January 1983

Liverpool 2 (Hodgson, Souness), West Ham United 1 (Allen).
Att: 23,953. Referee: M Heath.
Liverpool: Grobbelaar, Neal, Kennedy, Lawrenson, Johnston (Whelan), Hansen, Dalglish, Lee, Rush, Hodgson, Souness.
West Ham United: Parkes, Cowie, Gallagher, Bonds, Martin, Devonshire, Van der Elst, Goddard, Clark, Allen, Pike.

1983/84

Round Two first leg 4th October 1983

Bury 1 (Madden), West Ham United 2 (Goddard, Orr). Att: 8,050. Referee: M Heath. Bury: Brown, Gardner, Pashley (Coleman), Carrodus, Hilton, Bramhall, Potts, Madden, Spence, Jakub, Deacy. West Ham United: Parkes, Stewart, Walford (Orr), Bonds, Martin, Devonshire, Whitton, Goddard, Swindlehurst, Brooking, Pike.

Round Two second leg 25th October 1983

West Ham United 10 (Cottee 4, Martin, Brooking 2, Devonshire 2, Stewart), Bury 0. Att: 10.896. Referee: D Letts. West Ham United: Parkes, Stewart, Walford, Bonds (Orr), Martin, Devonshire, Allen, Cottee, Swindlehurst, Brooking, Pike. Bury: Brown, Gardner, Pashley, Coleman, Hilton, Bramhall, Potts, Entwhistle, Spence, Jakub, Deacy.

Teenager Tony Cottee led the massacre of Bury with four goals in this second round match at Upton Park. With midfield stars Trevor Brooking and Alan Devonshire scoring two apiece, West Ham went on to their biggest ever win, watched by their smallest-ever crowd for a home cup tie.

Leading 2-1 from the first leg, the Hammers soon put the issue beyond doubt when Swindlehurst headed down for Cottee to whip the ball home after only two minutes.

Five minutes later Bury should have drawn level after being awarded a penalty but Bramhall's spot kick rebounded off a post.

Alvin Martin rose to make it 2-0, and after 23 minutes Bonds released Brooking on the left and the England forward dummied past two defenders before squeezing the ball inside the far post. Ten minutes later Bonds headed on a cross for Cottee to dive and force the ball home.

Cottee completed his hat-trick five minutes later with a superb header from Paul Allen's cross and then Brooking made it 5-0 before Cottee got Hammers sixth after Martin headed on Devonshire's cross.

Swindlehurst put Devonshire through for goal number seven, then Stewart got the eighth from a penalty after Devonshire had been fouled. Nine minutes from time Brooking made it 9-0 with a deflected shot from the edge of the penalty area and the fans cries of "We want ten" were rewarded when Devonshire flicked home Brooking's pass five minutes from time.

Round Three 8th November 1983

West Ham United 1 (Swindlehurst), Brighton & Hove Albion 0. Att: 17,082. Referee: M Scott. West Ham United: Parkes, Stewart, Lampard, Walford, Martin, Devonshire, Orr, Cottee, Swindlehurst, Brooking, Pike. Brighton & Hove Albion: Corrigan, Ramsey, Pearce, Grealish, Young E, Gatting, O'Reagan, Young A (Smith), Ryan, Connor, Howlett, Smith.

Round Four 30th November 1983

West Ham United 2 (Mountfield (og), Pike), Everton 2 (Reid, Sheedy). Att: 19,782. Referee: A Gunn. West Ham United: Parkes, Stewart, Lampard, Walford, Martin, Devonshire, Whitton, Cottee (Orr), Swindlehurst, Brooking, Pike. Everton: Southall, Stevens, Ratcliffe, Mountfield, Higgins, Reid, Irvine, Heath Sharp, King, Sheedy.

Round Four replay 6th December 1983

Everton 2 (King, Sheedy) West Ham United 0. Att: 21,609. Referee: T Mills. Everton: Southall, Stevens, Ratcliffe, Mountfield, Higgins, Reid, Irvine, Heath Sharp, King, Sheedy. West Ham United: Parkes, Stewart, Lampard, Walford, Martin, Orr, Whitton, Cottee (Dickens), Swindlehurst, Brooking, Pike.

1984/85

Round Two first leg 25th September 1984

Bristol City 2 (Morgan, Walsh), West Ham United 2 (Cottee, Walford). Att: 15,894. Referee: V Callow. Bristol City: Shaw, Stevens, Newman, Phillipson-Masters, Halliday, Walsh, Hirst, Crawford, Pritchard, Morgan, Riley. West Ham United: McAlister, Stewart, Walford, Allen, Martin, Gale, Bonds, Goddard, Cottee, Dickens, Pike.

Round Two second leg 9th October 1984

West Ham United 6 (Cottee 2, Goddard 2, Whitton, Walford), Bristol City 1 (Walsh). Att: 11,376. Referee: K Baker. West Ham United: McAlister, Stewart, Walford, Allen, Martin, Gale, Whitton, Goddard, Cottee, Bonds (Barnes), Pike. Bristol City: Shaw, Stevens, Newman, Curle, Phillipson-Masters, Riley, Pritchard, Ritchie (Smith), Morgan, Walsh, Crawford.

Round Three 31st October 1984

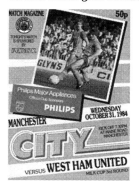

Manchester City 0, West Ham United 0. Att: 20.510. Referee: D Hutchinson. Manchester City: Williams, May, Power, Reid, McCarthy, Phillips, Smith (Beckford), Baker, Cunningham, Wilson, Kinsey. West Ham United: McAlister, Stewart, Walford, Allen, Martin, Gale, Whitton (Orr), Barnes, Cottee, Bonds, Pike.

Round Three replay 6th November 1984

West Ham United 1 (Whitton), Manchester City 2 (Cunningham, Kinsey). Att: 17,461. Referee: T Bune. West Ham United: McAlister, Stewart, Walford, Allen, Martin, Orr (Dickens), Whitton, Goddard, Cottee, Bonds, Pike. Manchester City: Williams, May, Power, Reid, McCarthy, Phillips, Smith, McNab, Cunningham, Wilson, Kinsey.

1985/86

Round Two first leg 24th September 1985

West Ham United 3 (Cottee, McAvennie, Stewart), Swansea Town 0. Att: 9,282. Referee: A Gunn. West Ham United: Parkes, Stewart, Walford, Gale, Martin, Devonshire, Ward, McAvennie, Dickens, Cottee, Orr. Swansea Town: Rimmer, Lewis, Sullivan, Price, Stevenson, Marustic, Hutchinson, Randell, Turner, Harrison, Pascoe.

Ex-Hammer John Bond was the Swans' manager and was looking for his Third Division side to make a good impression on his return to Upton Park. There were no goals in the first half but both sides made their contribution to the entertainment.

Three minutes after the interval West Ham took the lead when Alan Dickens provided the opportunity for Tony Cottee to score. On 56 minutes Frank McAvennie beat goalkeeper Rimmer with a well-directed header into the top corner of the net. A minute from the end Dickens was fouled in the area and from the spot it was Stewart who converted the penalty. The Hammers were pleased to take a three-goal lead to the second leg.

Round Two second leg 8th October 1985

Swansea Town 2 (Waddle, Randell), West Ham United 3 (Stewart 2, Cottee). Att: 3,584. Referee: R Groves.
Swansea Town: Hughes, Sharp, Sullivan, Price, McHale, Harrison, Hutchinson, Randell, Turner, Waddle (Stevenson), Pascoe.
West Ham United: Parkes, Stewart, Walford, Gale, Martin, Devonshire, Ward, McAvennie (Parris), Dickens, Cottee, Orr.

Round Three 29th October 1985

Manchester United 1 (Whiteside), West Ham United 0. Att: 32,057. Referee: F Roberts.
Manchester United: Bailey, Duxbury (Brazil), Albiston, Whiteside, Moran, Hogg, McGrath Olsen, Hughes, Stapleton, Barnes.
West Ham United: Parkes, Stewart, Walford, Gale, Martin, Devonshire, Ward, McAvennie, Dickens (Parris), Cottee, Orr.

1986/87

Round Two first leg 23rd September 1986

Preston North End 1 (Allardyce), West Ham United 1 (Ward). Att: 13,153. Referee: T Mills.
Preston North End: Brown, Bulmer, McAteer, Atkins, Jones, Allardyce, Williams, Clark, Thomas, Hildersley, Brazil.
West Ham United: Parkes, Stewart, Parris, Gale, Martin, Walford, Ward, McAvennie, Pike, Cottee, Orr.

Round Two second leg 7th October 1986

West Ham United 4 (Cottee, 3, Dickens), Preston North End 1 (Williams). Att: 12,742. Referee: V Callow.
West Ham United: Parkes, Stewart, Parris, Keen, Hilton, Walford, Ward, McAvennie, Dickens (Bonds), Cottee, Orr.
Preston North End: Kelly, McNeil, Bennett, Chapman (Saunders), Jones, Atkins, Williams, McAteer, Thomas (Allatt), Hildersley, Brazil.

The teams had drawn 1-1 in the first leg at Deepdale and within 12 minutes the Hammers went ahead. Ray Stewart hit a fierce drive and Tony Cottee netted from the rebound.

Then in the 26th minute the Lancashire team equalised when Williams scored after a goalmouth scramble. The margin was restored after an hour when Alan Dickens scored from close range. Preston then missed the best chance of the game when Thomas put the ball outside the post with only goalkeeper Parkes to beat. After another fine movement

Cottee scored again on 76 minutes. Seven minutes later the striker celebrated his England call up when he completed his hat-trick. With five minutes remaining Hammers legend Billy Bonds came on as sub to a huge reception. Due to injury this was his first appearance for 18 months.

Round Three 29th October 1986

Watford 2 (Jackett, Bardsley), West Ham United 3 (Goddard, Dickens, Ward).
Att: 17,523. Referee: J Bray.
Watford: Sherwood, Bardsley, Rostron, Richardson, Terry, McClelland, Sterling, Sinnott, Allen, Jackett, Barnes.
West Ham United: Parkes, Stewart, Parris, Gale, Hilton (Walford), Devonshire, Ward, Goddard, Dickens, Cottee, Orr.

Round Four 18th November 1986

West Ham United 1 (Cottee), Oxford United 0.
Att: 20,530.
Referee: H Taylor.
West Ham United: Parkes, Walford (Bonds), Parris, Gale, Hilton, Devonshire, Ward, McAvennie, Dickens, Cottee, Keen.
Oxford United: Hardwick, Langan, Slatter, Phillips, Briggs (Dreyer), Shotton, Houghton, Aldridge, Leworthy, Reck, Brock.

Quarter-final 27th January 1987

West Ham United 1 (Cottee), Tottenham Hotspur 1 (Allen).
Att: 29,477, Referee: B Stevens.
West Ham United: Parkes, Walford, Parris, Hilton, Martin, Devonshire, Ward, McAvennie, Dickens, Cottee, Robson.
Tottenham Hotspur: Clemence, Thomas D, Thomas M, Ardiles, Gough, Mabbutt, Allen C, Allen P, Waddle, Hoddle, Claesen.

Quarter-final replay 2nd February 1987

Tottenham Hotspur 5 (Claesen, Hoddle, Allen C 3), West Ham United 0.
Att: 41,995.
Referee: V Callow.
Tottenham Hotspur: Clemence, Thomas D, Thomas M, Ardiles, Gough, Mabbuttt, Allen C, Allen P, Waddle, Hoddle, Claesen.
West Ham United: Parkes, Bonds, Parris (Hilton), Gale, Martin, Devonshire, Ward, McAvennie, Orr, Cottee, Robson.

1987/88

Round Two first leg 22nd September 1987

Barnsley 0, West Ham United 0.
Att: 10,330.
Referee: A Seville.
Barnsley: Baker, Joyce, Cross, Thomas, Gray, Futcher, Wylde, Agnew, Lowndes, MacDonald, Clarke (Beresford).
West Ham United: McAlister, Potts (McQueen), Parris, Strodder, Martin, Brady, Ward, McAvennie, Ince, Cottee, Robson.

Round Two second leg 6th October 1987

West Ham United 2 (Keen, Robson), Barnsley 5 (Agnew 2, Beresford, Lowndes, MacDonald).
Att: 12,403. Referee: K Morton.

West Ham United: McAlister, Parris (Dickens), McQueen (Hilton), Strodder, Martin, Brady, Ward, Keen, Ince, Cottee, Robson.
Barnsley: Baker, Joyce, Cross, Thomas, Gray, Futcher, Beresford, Agnew, Lowndes, MacDonald, Broddle.

An embarrassing exit for the Hammers as they crashed out of the League Cup after leading 2-0 at half-time. It had all started brightly as Stewart Robson put West Ham ahead after 3 minutes when he fired home a through ball from Keen.

On the half hour Futcher handled and the referee had no hesitation in awarding a penalty. Tony Cottee stepped up and hit it firmly but goalkeeper Baker parried the ball. Kevin Keen however responded well as he darted in to net the loose ball.

Early in the second half the Hammers Alvin Martin conceded a penalty for pushing. Agnew made no mistake from the spot and 20 minutes later he fired in a free kick to equalise.

In extra-time Beresford chipped a free kick over the wall to put Barnsley ahead. Then as half-time beckoned Futcher set up Lowndes who easily scored. Six minutes into the second period Broddle outpaced the Hammers defence to leave MacDonald who made no mistake in scoring the fifth. Both Paul Hilton and Cottee went close for West Ham after that but the tie ended with a chorus of boos from the home faithful.

1988/89

Round Two first leg 27th September 1988

Sunderland 0, West Ham United 3 (Kelly, 2, Rosenior). Att: 13,691. Referee: G Aplin. Sunderland: Hesford, Kay, Agboola, Bennett (Gray), Macphail, Doyle, Owers, Armstrong, Gates, Gabbiadini, Pascoe. West Ham United: McKnight, Parris, Dicks, Hilton, Martin (Potts), Ince, Ward, Kelly, Rosenior, Dickens, Robson.

Round Two second leg 12th October 1988

West Ham United: 2 (Kelly, Dickens), Sunderland 1 (Gabbiadini). Att: 10,558. Referee: A Seville. West Ham United: McKnight, Potts, Dicks, Gale, Hilton, Devonshire (Keen), Ward, Kelly, Parris, Dickens, Ince. Sunderland: Hesford, Gray, Agboola, Ord, MacPhail, Doyle (Lemon), Owers, Armstrong, Gates, Gabbiadini, Pascoe (Ogilvie).

Round Three 1st November 1988

West Ham United 5 (Martin, 2, Stewart, Rosenior, Keen), Derby County 0. Att: 14,226. Referee: K Morton. West Ham United: McKnight, Stewart, Dicks, Gale, Martin, Keen, Ward, Kelly (Brady), Rosenior, Dickens, Ince. Derby County: Shilton, Sage, Forsyth, Williams, Hindmarch, Blades, McMinn, Gee (Micklewhite), Goddard, Hebberd, Callaghan (Cross).

Languishing in the lower reaches of the league, the Hammers brought smiles to their suffering fans by hitting five goals past England goalkeeper Shilton. Both Paul Ince and David Kelly went close in the first half but the Hammers did not go ahead until a minute from half-time. A free kick from Mark Ward gave defender Alvin Martin the chance to power a header past Shilton in the Derby goal. On 53 minutes West Ham went further ahead as Ray Stewart made no mistake from the penalty spot. After 69 minutes Kevin Keen and Dickens set up Leroy Rosenior who blasted the third.

Alvin Martin scored his second of the match in the 79th minute when Tony Gale nodded back a corner kick from Ward. A minute from time the impressive Ince gave a through ball to Keen who slotted home the fifth goal.

Round Four 30th November 1988

West Ham United 4 (Ince 2, Staunton (og), Gale), Liverpool 1 (Aldridge). Att: 26,971. Referee: J Ashworth. West Ham United: McKnight, Potts, Dicks, Gale, Martin, Devonshire, Brady, Kelly, Rosenior, Dickens, Ince. Liverpool: Hooper, Ablett, Venison, Nicol (Watson), Whelan, Spackman, Beardsley, Aldridge, Saunders, Houghton, McMahon (Durnin).

West Ham were struggling in the League when they met the Merseysiders but under the lights at Upton Park the Hammers are a different proposition as many opponents have discovered.

From the start the Hammers were confident and their passing was sharp. Wave after wave of attacks flooded towards the North Bank goal. Then in the 20th minute Brady sent over a curling cross which was spectacularly volleyed into the net by Paul Ince.

Three minutes later Liverpool were stunned when Ince again dashed in to head Devonshire's corner wide of Hooper. After 34 minutes however, Liverpool were back in the game when referee Ashworth awarded them a penalty. Alvin Martin was adjudged to have held Aldridge, who took the kick himself and beat McKnight.

On 57 minutes an aimless cross by Kelly dropped into the Liverpool penalty area and Staunton decided to head it back to goalkeeper Hooper but misdirected his effort into the net.

Liverpool became disheartened and their misery was complete after 76 minutes. A free kick was awarded to West Ham and Tony Gale curled the ball over the wall and beyond Hooper's grasping fingertips. The 4-1 scoreline stunned the footballing world, for it was the Reds heaviest cup defeat since February 1939. It was also a night to saviour for the Hammers ecstatic fans.

Quarter-final 18th January 1989

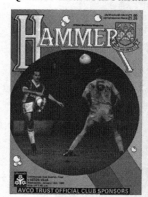

West Ham United 2 (Ince, Kelly), Aston Villa 1 (Platt). Att: 30,110. Referee: J Martin. West Ham United: McKnight, Potts, Dicks, Gale, Strodder, Devonshire, Brady, Kelly, Rosenior, Dickens (Ward), Ince. Aston Villa: Spink, Price, Gray S, Gage, Mountfield, Keown, Gray A, Platt, McInally, Cowans, Daley (Olney).

Semi-final first leg 12th February 1989

West Ham United 0, Luton Town 3 (Harford, Wegerle, Wilson). Att: 24,602. Referee: G Courtney. West Ham United: McKnight, Potts, Dicks, Gale, Martin, Devonshire, Ward, Dickens, Rosenior, Brady (Kelly), Ince. Luton Town: Sealey, Breacker, Grimes, Preece, Foster, Beaumont, Wilson, Wegerle, Harford, Hill, Black.

Two howlers by Allen McKnight in the Hammer's goal and a below-par team performance led to the crowd singing "what a load of rubbish" and deserting the stands well before the end of the game.

Semi-final second leg 1st March 1989

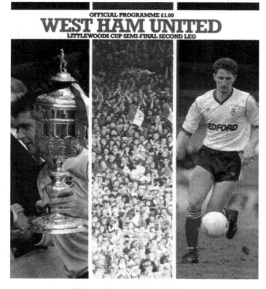

Luton Town 2 (Harford, Wegerle), West Ham United 0.
Att: 12,020. Referee: D Axcell.
Luton Town: Sealey, Breacker, Grimes, Preece, Foster, Beaumont, Wilson, Wegerle, Harford, Hill, Black.
West Ham United: Parkes, Potts, Dicks, Gale, Martin, Kelly, Ward, Parris, Slater, Brady, Ince.

1989/90

Round Two first leg 19th September 1989

Birmingham City 1 (Sprosson), West Ham United 2 (Allen, Slater).
Att: 10,987. Referee: D Allison.
Birmingham City: Thomas, Ashley, Matthewson, Atkins, Sprosson, Overson, Peer, Bailey, Gordon (Sturridge), Gleghorn, Hopkins.
West Ham United: Parkes, Potts, Dicks, Gale, Martin, Keen, Ward (Brady), Slater, Allen, Dolan, Parris.

Round Two second leg 4th October 1989

West Ham United 1 (Dicks), Birmingham City 1 (Atkins).
Att: 12,187. Referee: A Gunn.
West Ham United: Parkes, Potts, Dicks, Gale, Martin, Keen, Allen, Slater, Dolan (Kelly), Ward (Brady), Parris.
Birmingham City: Thomas, Ashley, Matthewson, Atkins, Sprosson, Overson, Tait (Peer), Bailey, Sturridge (Roberts), Gleghorn, Hopkins.

Round Three 25th October 1989
Aston Villa 0, West Ham United 0.

Att: 20,989. Referee: G Courtney.
Aston Villa: Spink, Price, Gage, Birch (Osmondroyd), Mountfield, Nielson, Daley (Blake), Platt, Olney, Cowans, Gray.
West Ham United: Parkes, Potts, Dicks, Strodder, Martin, Keen, Brady (Kelly), Slater, Dolan, Allen, Parris.

Round Three replay 8th November 1989

West Ham United 1 (Dicks), Aston Villa 0 Att: 23,833. Referee: D Hutchinson.
West Ham United: Parkes, Potts, Dicks, Strodder, Martin, Keen, Brady, Slater, Dolan, Ward, Parris.
Aston Villa: Spink, Price, Gage (Comyn), McGrath, Mountfield, Nielson, Daley (Callaghan), Platt, Olney, Cowans, Ormondroyd.

Round Four 22nd November 1989

West Ham United 1 (Allen), Wimbledon 0 Att: 24,746. Referee: A Buksh.
West Ham United: Parkes, Potts, Dicks, Strodder, Martin, Keen (Fashanu), Brady, Slater, Allen, Ward, Parris (Devonshire).
Wimbledon: Siegers, Joseph, Phelan, Ryan, Young, Curle, Fairweather, Miller (Cork), Cotterill, Sanchez (Scales), Wise.

Quarter-final 17th January 1990

West Ham United 1 (Dicks), Derby County 1 (Saunders).
Att: 25,035. Referee: V Callow.
West Ham United: Parkes, Potts, Dicks, Parris, Martin, Gale, Brady, Kelly, Rosenior (Slater), Allen, Keen.
Derby County: Shilton, Sage, Forsyth, Williams, Wright, Hindmarch, Pickering, Saunders, Ramage (Patterson), Hebberd, Cross (Francis).

Quarter-final replay 24th January 1990

Derby County 0, West Ham United 0. Att: 22,510. Referee: J Worrall.
Derby County: Taylor, Sage, Forsyth, Williams, Wright, Hindmarch, Patterson, Saunders, Harford (Francis), Hebberd, McCord (Briscoe).
West Ham United: Parkes, Strodder, McQueen, Parris, Martin, Gale, Brady (Milne), Kelly, Slater, Robson (Devonshire), Keen.

Quarter-final second replay 31st January 1990

West Ham United 2 (Slater, Keen), Derby County 1 (Saunders). Att: 25,166. Referee: K Barratt.
West Ham United: Parkes, Potts (McQueen), Dicks, Parris, Martin, Gale, Brady, Kelly, Slater, Robson, Keen.
Derby County: Taylor, Sage, Forsyth, Williams, Patterson, Davidson, Francis (Ramage), Saunders, Harford, Hebberd, Briscoe.

Semi-final first leg 14th February 1990

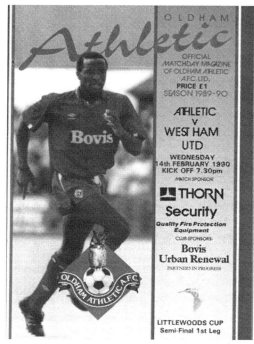

Oldham Athletic 6 (Adams, Ritchie, 2, Barrett, Holden, Palmer), West Ham United 0.
Att: 19,263. Referee: L Shapter.
Oldham Athletic: Hallworth, Irwin, Barlow, Henry, Marshall, Barrett, Adams, Ritchie, Palmer, Milligan, Holden.
West Ham United: Parkes, Robson, Dicks, Parris, Martin, Gale, Brady, Slater, Strodder (Devonshire), Kelly, Keen.

The 6,000 rain soaked West Ham supporters were badly let down by the woeful display of their team. Although the plastic pitch was an advantage to the home team there was no excuse for the total surrender and poor defending that led to this humiliating defeat.

On 11 minutes Adams plays a one-two with Ritchie before firing home the first goal. Ritchie carried the ball from his own half to hit a low drive past Parkes after 19 minutes. After half an hour Palmer fed Barrett who prodded home Oldham's third.

A minute into the second half saw the Latics go four up after a cross from Irwin found Holden who picked his spot from 8 yards. The Hammers briefly rallied after

Alan Devonshire came on as a substitute but on 69 minutes Palmer stabbed the ball past Parkes following a Holden corner. The rout was complete nine minutes later as Holden sent over a cross to Ritchie who headed home from two yards. Oldham had been superior in every department and the Hammers were not able to cope with the bombardment.

Semi-final second leg 7th March 1990

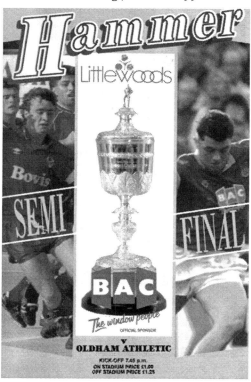

West Ham United 3 (Martin, Dicks, Kelly), Oldham Athletic 0.
Att: 15,431. Referee: T Holbrook.
West Ham United: Miklosko, Slater, Dicks, Parris, Martin, Gale, Brady (McQueen), Allen, Rosenior, Kelly, Keen.
Oldham Athletic: Hallworth, Irwin, Barlow, Henry, Barrett, Warhurst, Adams, Palmer, Marshall, Milligan, Holden.

"You only score on plastic" sang the Hammer's fans, but the 6 goal deficit proved too much despite all-out attacking play.

1990/91

Round Two first leg 26th September 1990

West Ham United 3 (Dicks, Keen, Quinn), Stoke City 0. Att: 15,870. Referee: B Hill.
West Ham United: Miklosko, Potts, Dicks, Foster, Martin, Keen, Bishop, Quinn, Slater, Allen (Parris), Morley.
Stoke City: Fox, Butler, Statham (Fowler), Beeston, Blake, Sandford, Kennedy, Evans, Kelly (Thomas), Biggins, Ware.

Round Two second leg 10th October 1990

Stoke City 1 (Evans), West Ham United 2 (Allen 2). Att: 8,411. Referee: N Midgeley.
Stoke City: Fox, Butler, Carr, Ware, Blake, Sandford, Scott, Ellis, Evans, Biggins, Kevan (Boughey).
West Ham United: Miklosko, Potts, Dicks, Foster, Martin, Keen (Gale), Bishop, Parris, Quinn (McAvennie), Allen, Morley.

Round Three 31st October 1990

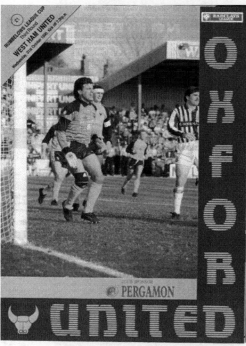

Oxford United 2 (Foyle, Magilton), West Ham United 1 (Morley).
Att: 7,528, Referee: V Callow.
Oxford United: Kee, Robinson, Evans, Lewis, Foster, Melville, Magilton, Stein (Penney), Foyle, Morgan, Simpson.
West Ham United: Miklosko, Rush, Keen, Foster, Martin, Parris, Bishop, Quinn, Slater, Allen, Morley.

1991/92

Round Two first leg 24th September 1991

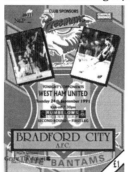

Bradford City 1 (Leonard), West Ham United 1 (Small).
Att: 7,034. Referee: R Nixon.
Bradford City: Tomlinson, Mitchell, Dowson, James, Leonard, Gardner, Babb, Duxbury, Turpey, Tinnion, Reid.
West Ham United: Miklosko, Brown, Parris, Thomas, Foster, Breacker, Bishop, Slater, Small, Potts, Morley (Gale).

Round Two second leg 9th October 1991

West Ham United 4 (Keen, Morley, Parris, Small), Bradford City 0.
Att: 17,232. Referee: M James.
West Ham United: Miklosko, Breacker, Thomas, Gale, Foster, Parris, Bishop, Slater, Small (McAvennie), Keen, Morley.
Bradford City: Tomlinson, Mitchell, Dowson, James, Oliver, Gardner, Babb, Duxbury, Torpey (Leonard), Tinnion, Morgan (McCarthy).

After a 1-1 draw in the first leg Third Division Bradford were looking for a cup upset. West Ham had other ideas and ran out easy winners after scoring four times without reply. After 9 minutes Stuart Slater burst down the wing and put in a cross where Kevin Keen raced in to fire a drive past Tomlinson in the Bradford goal. On 36 minutes Tim Breacker came down the line and chipped the ball to the far post where Trevor Morley headed home. The Bantams fought back and Ludek Miklosko saved well from a low 25-yarder from James. Ten

minutes into the second half and it was George Parris playing a one-two with Small before making it 3-0.

After Mitchell Thomas hit the post for the Hammers they scored again after Trevor Morley headed back to Small who then headed home. Frank McAvennie came on for his first appearance of the season just a few minutes from time.

Round Three 29th October 1991

Sheffield United 0, West Ham United 2 (McAvennie, Small).
Att: 11,144. Referee: G Courtney.
Sheffield United: Kite, Pemberton, Cowan, Gannon, Gayle, Beesley, Bryson (Mendonca), Holroyd, Agana, Bradshaw (Lake), Whitehouse.
West Ham United: Miklosko, Breacker, Thomas, Gale (Allen), Potts, Parris, Bishop, McAvennie, Small, Keen, Slater.

Round Four 4th December 1991

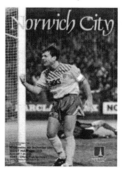

Norwich City 2 (Fleck 2), West Ham United 1 (Small)
Att: 16,325. Referee: K Morton.
Norwich City: Gunn, Phillips, Bowen, Sutton, Blades (Crook), Goss, Ullathorne, Fleck, Newman, Sherwood, Beckford (Fox).
West Ham United: Miklosko, Breacker, Thomas, Gale, Potts, Parris, Bishop, McAvennie, Small, Allen, Slater.

1992/93

Round Two first leg 23rd September 1992

West Ham United 0, Crewe Alexandra 0.
Att: 6,891. Referee: A Maile.
West Ham United: Miklosko, Breacker, Thomas, Potts, Martin, Allen M, Robson, Butler, Morley, Allen C, Keen (Small).
Crewe Alexandra: Greygoose, McKearney, Whalley, Wilson, Carr, Macauley, Gardiner, Garvey, Clarkson (Naylor), Harvey (Hughes), Walters.

Round Two second leg 7th October 1992

Crewe Alexandra 2 (Naylor, Hignett), West Ham United 0.
Att: 5,427.
Referee: T Lunt.
Crewe Alexandra: Greygoose, McKearney, Whalley, Wilson, Carr, Macauley, Hignett, Naylor, Clarkson (Garvey), Harvey (Gardiner), Walters.
West Ham United: Miklosko, Breacker, Dicks, Potts, Martin, Allen M, Robson, Butler, Morley, Allen C, Keen.

1993/94

Round Two first leg 22nd September 1993

West Ham United 5 (Morley 2, Chapman 2, Burrows), Chesterfield 1 (Norris).
Att: 12,823. Referee: I Borrett.
West Ham United: Miklosko, Rowland, Burrows, Potts, Gale, Bishop, Gordon, Morley, Chapman, Holmes, Marsh.
Chesterfield: Leonard, Hebberd, Carr C, Brien, Carr D, McGuigan, Dyche, Norris, Jules (Davies), Cash (Knowles), Curtis.

This first leg tie saw the Hammers all but through to the next round as they demolished the threat of the Third Division team.

As early as the 6th minute new boy Lee Chapman (on his home debut) was brought down for a penalty. This led Trevor Morley to convert from the spot. On 15 minutes West Ham scored again from a Chapman header. After half an hour another new boy David Burrows drilled home following a free kick from Mattie Holmes. The Hammers were well on top at this stage and the Chesterfield goal was peppered with shots from Dale Gordon, Morley and Chapman.

However 10 minutes after the interval Chesterfield pulled one back. McGuigan nodded forward to leave Norris to volley past Miklosko. After 65 minutes a lob from Morley found Chapman who scored with a close range header. Four minutes later Morley played a one-two with Mike Marsh before picking his spot for Hammers' fifth.

Round Two second leg 5th October 1993

Chesterfield 0, West Ham United 2 (Allen, Boere). Att: 4,890. Referee: G Singh. Chesterfield: Marples, Hebberd, Carr C, Brien, Madden, Dennis, Dyche (Bettney), Norris (Taylor), Davies, Curtis, Jules. West Ham United: Miklosko, Breacker, Burrows, Potts, Gale, Bishop, Butler (Allen), Morley, Chapman (Boere), Marsh, Holmes.

Round Three 27th October 1993

Nottingham Forest 2 (Black, Collymore), West Ham United 1 (Morley). Att: 17,857. Referee: G Pooley. Nottingham Forest: Wright, Laws, Pearce, Crosby, Chettle, Stone, Phillips, Gemmell, Glover (Webb), Collymore, Black. West Ham United: Miklosko, Breacker, Burrows, Potts, Martin, Bishop, Butler (Allen), Morley, Chapman, Marsh, Holmes.

1994/95

Round Two first leg 20th September 1994

Walsall 2 (Watkins, Potts (og)), West Ham United 1 (Ntamark (og)). Att: 5,994. Referee: P Harrison. Walsall: Wood, Evans, Rogers, Watkiss, Marsh, Palmer (Ryder), O'Connor, Peer, Lightbourne, Wilson, Ntamark (Mehew). West Ham United: Miklosko, Breacker, Rowland, Potts, Martin, Allen (Chapman), Moncur, Marsh, Hutchison, Rush (Whitbread), Cottee.

Round Two second leg 5th October 1994

West Ham United 2 (Hutchison, Moncur), Walsall 0. Att: 13,553. Referee: J Holbrook. West Ham United: Miklosko, Breacker, Rowland, Potts, Moncur (Brown), Allen, Bishop, Marsh, Hutchison, Whitbread, Chapman. Walsall: Wood, Rider, Rogers, Watkiss, Marsh (Ntamark), Palmer, O'Connor (Evans), Peer, Lightbourne, Wilson, Mehew.

Round Three 26th October 1994

West Ham United 1 (Hutchison), Chelsea 0. Att: 18,815. Referee: K Cooper. West Ham United: Miklosko, Breacker, Dicks, Potts, Martin, Allen, Bishop, Marsh, Hutchison, Rush, Cottee. Chelsea: Kharin, Kjeldberg, Johnsen, Spackman, Newton, Barness, Hall (Hopkin), Rocastle, Peacock (Lee), Wise, Shipperley.

Round Four 30th November 1994

West Ham United 1 (Cottee), Bolton Wanderers 3 (McGinlay 2, Whitbread (og)). Att: 18,190. Referee: P Durkin. West Ham United: Miklosko, Brown, Dicks, Potts, Whitbread, Rush, Bishop, Holmes (Morley), Moncur, Boere, Cottee. Bolton Wanderers: Branagan, Green, Phillips, McAteer, Coleman, Stubbs, Lee (Patterson), Sneakes, Paatelainen, McGinlay, Thompson.

1995/96

Round Two first leg 20th September 1995

Bristol, Rovers 0, West Ham United 1 (Moncur). Att: 7,103. Referee: K Cooper. Bristol Rovers: Parkin, Pritchard, Gurney, Browning, Wright, Tilson, Skinner, Miller, Stewart, Channing (Wyatt), Taylor. West Ham United: Miklosko, Breacker, Dicks, Potts, Martin, Bishop, Moncur, Dowie (Rieper), Cottee, Lazaridis, Slater (Williamson).

Round Two second leg 4th October 1995
West Ham United 3 (Dicks, Bishop, Cottee), Bristol Rovers 0.

Att: 15,375. Referee: R Gifford. West Ham United: Miklosko, Breacker, Dicks, Potts, Rieper, Bishop, Moncur, Dowie, Cottee, Slater, Hughes. Bristol Rovers: Parkin, Pritchard, Gurney, Browning, Wright, Tilson, Sterling, Paul, Stewart, Skinner, Channing (Davis).

The first half belonged to Bristol but they missed their chances to score. Channing and Browning blew opportunities while Pritchard hit the post with a 30-yard piledriver. They did not have it all their own way as Julian Dicks was unlucky when he headed a Hughes centre a fraction wide.

Five minutes into the second half saw the Hammers go ahead.
Cottee was fouled in the box and Julian Dicks buried the resultant penalty. Within a minute Ian Bishop stunned Rovers with a shot which thundered through a pack of players to nestle in the net. Channing and Stewart then

squandered chances before Tony Cottee grabbed his first goal of the season from a pass from Stuart Slater to give a comfortable 3-0 scoreline.

Round Three 25th October 1995

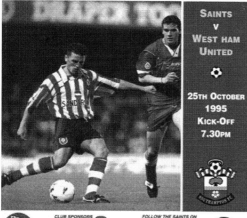

Southampton 2 (Watson, Shipperley), West Ham United 1 (Cottee).
Att: 11,059. Referee: P Danson,
Southampton: Beasant, Dodd, Benali, Venison, Hall, Monkou, Le Tissier, Watson, Shipperley, Hughes, Heaney.
West Ham United: Miklosko, Potts, Dicks, Rieper, Martin, Bishop, Moncur, Dowie, Cottee, Slater, Hughes.

1996/97

Round Two first leg 18th September 1996

Barnet 1 (Simpson), West Ham United 1 (Cottee).
Att: 3,849. Referee: M Riley.
Barnet: Taylor, Primus, Pardew, Howarth, McDonald, Wilson, Codner, Gale, Simpson (Tomlinson), Rattray (Campbell), Devine.
West Ham United: Mautone, Breacker (Lazaridis), Dicks, Rieper, Bilic, Bowen, Hughes, Bishop, Moncur (Lampard), Dowie, Cottee.

Round Two second leg 25th September 1996

West Ham United 1 (Bilic), Barnet 0.
Att: 15,264. Referee: C Wilkes.
West Ham United: Mautone, Breacker, Dicks, Rieper, Bilic, Moncur, Lazaridis (Ferdinand), Bishop, Dumitrescu, Dowie, Cottee (Jones).
Barnet: Taylor, Gale (Campbell), McDonald, Codner, Primus, Howarth, Rattray (Hodges), Hardyman (Tomlinson), Wilson, Devine, Pardew.

Round Three 23rd October 1996

West Ham United 4 (Dowie 2, Porfirio, Dicks), Nottingham Forest 1 (Cooper). Att: 19,402. Referee: D Elleray.
West Ham United: Miklosko, Bowen, Dicks, Rieper, Bilic, Lazaridis, Hughes, Bishop, Moncur, Dowie, Porfirio.
Nottingham Forest: Crossley, Haarland, Cooper, Blatherwich, Phillips, Gemmell, Bart-Williams, Woan, Roy, Lee, Saunders.

Portuguese destroyer Hugo Porfirio ran struggling Forest ragged with his electric pace and dazzling skills. The Hammers striker Iain Dowie had gone 11 games without scoring but he took just 13 minutes to score the opener as he thumped Porfirio's pass into the net from 6 yards. Midway through the first half Cooper equalised with a simple header from a cross from Saunders.

The Hammers then set about regaining the lead as both Stan Lazaridis and Dicks tested Crossley. In the second half there was only one team in it as Porfirio ran riot. He went close himself before putting a through ball to Dowie who placed a shot beyond the Forest 'keeper. Then 20 minutes later Dowie back-heeled the ball to Porfirio who lifted the ball over Crossley from 10 yards. With 18 minutes left Haarland wrestled over Lazaridis in the penalty area and Dicks blasted home the spot kick.

Round Four 27th November 1996

West Ham United 1 (Raducioiu), Stockport County 1 (Cavaco). Att: 20,061. Referee: M Bailey.
West Ham United: Mikloso, Breacker, Dicks, Potts, Bilic, Lazaridis (Dumitrescu), Hughes, Bishop, Lampard, Dowie, Raducioiu.

Stockport County: Jones, Connelly, Gannon, Flynn, Todd, Durkan (Dinning), Bennett, Marsden, Jeffers (Cavaco), Armstrong, Angell.

Round Four replay 18th December 1996

Stockport County 2 (Dowie (og), Angell), West Ham United 1 (Dicks). Att: 9,834. Referee: U Rennie.
Stockport County: Jones, Connelly, Flynn, Gannon, Todd, Durkan, Bennett, Marsden, Cavaco (Dinning), Armstrong, Angell.
West Ham United: Miklosko, Bowen, Dicks, Rieper, Bilic, Moncur, Hughes, Bishop, Dumitrescu, Dowie (Williamson), Porfirio.

On a rain soaked December night the signs were there for a giant killing. However it was the Hammers who scored first after 21 minutes. Moncur's shot went off Flynn for a corner which was taken by Dumetrescu. When the ball floated over Julian Dicks was on hand to head it home.

Within minutes County were level with a bizarre goal. Armstrong flicked on a header but incredibly, in an attempt to clear, Iain Dowie sent a pinpoint powerful header past a bewildered Miklosko for a ludicrous leveller.

Worse followed three minutes later when Bennett centred and Angell sent a looping header into the net. Just after that Bishop rattled the bar and Dowie put a shot wide. To complete Dowie's misery he then went off after suffering a broken ankle. Once again the Hammers were left in despair after losing to a lower League team in the cup.

1997/98

Round Two first leg 16th September 1997

Huddersfield Town 1 (Dyer), West Ham United 0.
Att: 8,525. Referee: C Wilkes.
Huddersfield Town: Francis, Jenkins, Martin (Baldry), Dyson, Gray, Edmondson, Dalton (Hurst), Makel, Stewart, Dyer, Burnett.
West Ham United: Miklosko, Breacker, Hughes, Unsworth, Ferdinand, Potts, Lampard, Berkovic, Kitson (Dowie), Hartson, Lomas.

Round Two second leg 29th September 1997

West Ham United 3 (Hartson 3), Huddersfield Town 0.
Att: 16,137. Referee: M Bodenham.
West Ham United: Miklosko, Breacker, Impey (Potts), Unsworth, Ferdinand, Pearce, Lampard, Dowie, Hartson, Berkovic, Lomas.
Huddersfield Town: Francis, Jenkins, Edmondson, Collins, Morrison, Gray, Edwards (Lawson), Makel (Burnett), Stewart, Payton, Dyer.

Round Three 15th October 1997

West Ham United 3 (Hartson, 2, Lampard), Aston Villa 0.
Att: 20,360. Referee: S Lodge.
West Ham United: Forrest, Breacker (Rowland), Impey, Potts, Ferdinand, Unsworth, Lampard, Dowie (Bishop), Hartson, Berkovic, Lomas.
Aston Villa: Bosnich, Nelson (Charles), Wright, Southgate (Grayson), Ehiogu, Scimeca, Taylor, Draper, Milosevic (Curcic), Collymore, Yorke.

Round Four 19th November 1997

West Ham United 4 (Lampard 3, Hartson), Walsall 1 (Watson).
Att: 17,463. Referee: D Orr.
West Ham United: Forrest, Breacker, Lomas, Unsworth, Ferdinand, Pearce, Moncur, Lampard, Hartson, Berkovic, Abou.
Walsall: Walker, Evans, Marsh (Ricketts), Viveash, Mountfield, Peron, Boli, Keister (Porter), Keates, Watson, Hodge.

A smart hat-trick from young Frank Lampard saw the Hammers roar into the last eight. In the 14th minute Lampard burst upon Berkovic's through ball and clipped a shot in off the far post. Minutes later John Hartson came through and slotted past Walker from a tight angle. Walsall bounced back when Peron and Boli both went close. Then right on half-time they got a goal back when Peron's corner was nodded on by Mountfield and Watson bundled the ball past Craig Forrest.

The Saddlers came out for the second half intent on an equaliser and Boli brought a good save from Forrest after sending in a sizzling 18 yarder. A pass from Eyal Berkovic after 72 minutes allowed Lampard to tuck a low shot past Walker, and minutes later he completed his hat-trick when he chipped over the advancing keeper.

Quarter-final 6th January 1998

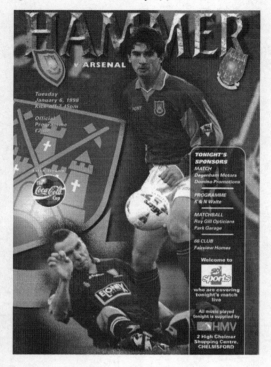

West Ham United 1 (Abou), Arsenal 2 (Wright, Overmars).
Att: 24,770. Referee: G Barber.
West Ham United: Forrest, Potts, Lazaridis, Unsworth, Ferdinand, Pearce (Rowland), Impey, Berkovic, Kitson (Abou), Hartson, Lampard.
Arsenal: Seaman, Grimaldi, Winterburn, Vieira, Bould, Keown, Parlour, Wright (Wreh), Petit, Bergkamp, Overmars (Hughes).

1998/99

Round Two first leg 15th September 1998

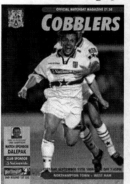

Northampton Town 2 (Freestone 2), West Ham United 0.
Att: 7,254. Referee: P Alcock.
Northampton Town: Woodham, Gibb, Parrish, Sampson, Warburton, Peer, Hunter (Hunt), Spedding, Freestone (Heggs), Corazzin (Wilkinson), Hill.
West Ham United: Hislop, Sinclair, Lazaridis, Potts, Pearce, Ruddock (Breacker), Lampard, Berkovic, Hartson, Wright, Moncur.

Round Two second leg 22nd September 1998

West Ham United 1 (Lampard), Northampton Town 0.
Att: 25,435. Referee: D Gallagher.
West Ham United: Hislop, Impey, Dicks, Potts, Ferdinand, Pearce, Keller, Lampard, Abou (Omoyinmi), Wright, Sinclair.
Northampton Town: Woodham, Gibb, Frain, Sampson, Warburton, Peer, Hunter (Spedding), Wilkinson, Freestone (Dobson), Parrish (Corazzin), Hill.

1999/2000

Round Three 13th October 1999
West Ham United 2 (Keller, Lampard), Bournemouth 0.
Att: 22,067. Referee: R Harris.
West Ham United: Hislop, Ferdinand, Stimac, Ruddock, Sinclair, Lampard, Foe, Cole, Keller, Wanchope (Kitson), Di Canio.
Bournemouth: Ovendale, Warren (Huck), Cox, Howe, Young, Mean, Broadhurst, Jorgenson (O 'Neill), Robinson, Fletcher, Stein.

Round Four 30th November 1999

Birmingham City 2 (Hyde, Grainger), West Ham United 3 (Lomas, Kitson, Cole).
Att: 17,728. Referee: G Poll.
Birmingham City: Poole, Bass, Rowett, Holdsworth, Johnson, Grainger, Hyde (Hughes), Holland, O'Connor, Purse, Johnston.
West Ham United: Hislop, Charles (Cole), Margas (Sinclair), Ruddock, Ferdinand, Keller, Lampard, Foe, Lomas, Di Canio, Wanchope (Kitson).

West Ham went through to the quarter-finals in a dramatic fashion by scoring twice inside the last 3 minutes. The Hammers were a goal down in 8 minutes after a run from Johnston found Hyde who lashed home. After 20 minutes the Hammers were level when Steve Lomas collected Frank Lampard's free kick and hit a rocket from 35 yards which went in beneath the right hand post. Just afterwards a mazy run from Paolo Di Canio left Wanchope with a good opportunity which he wasted. It was a costly miss as just after that the Blues took the lead when Grainger curled a free kick over the wall and into the net.

In the second half both Paul Kitson and Joe Cole came on as substitutes to liven up the play. With only two minutes to play Di Canio pulled the ball back for Kitson to grab the equaliser. Then with just six seconds left Cole half volleyed his first goal for the club and left Birmingham stunned.

Quarter-final 15th December 1999

The first game against Aston Villa was ordered to be replayed and the statistics removed from the record. Please see Appendix 2 "the Omoyinmi Affair" for a full account.

Quarter-final 11th January 2000

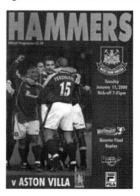

West Ham United 1 (Lampard), Aston Villa 3 (Taylor, 2, Joachim).
Att: 25,592. Referee: J Winter.
West Ham United: Hislop, Ferdinand, Potts (Ruddock), Stimac, Minto, Lomas, Lampard, Foe, Cole, Di Canio, Sinclair (Keller).
Aston Villa: James, Watson, Ehiogu, Southgate, Barry, Wright, Stone, Taylor, Boateng, Joachim, Merson (Vassell).

2000/01

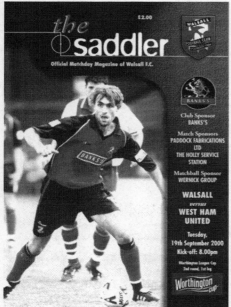

Round Two first leg 18th September 2000
Walsall 0, West Ham United 1 (Defoe).
Att: 5,435. Referee: S, Lodge.
Walsall: Walker, Brightwell, Aranalde, Tilson, Barras, Bukran, Hall (Angell), Keates, Leitao, Byfield, Matias.
West Ham United: Hislop, Potts, Winterburn, Stimac, Ferdinand, Pearce S, Lomas, Cole, Sinclair, Carrick, Keller (Defoe).

Round Two second leg 27th September 2000

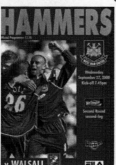

West Ham United 1 (Lomas), Walsall 1 (Leitao).
Att: 11,963. Referee: A D'Urso.
West Ham United: Hislop, Margas, Winterburn, Stimac, Lampard (Potts), Pearce S, Lomas, Cole, DiCanio, Carrick, Kanoute.
Walsall: Walker, Brightwell, Aranalde, Tilson, Barras (Roper), Bukran, Hall (Wright), Bennett, Leitao, Angell (Douglas), Matias.

Round Three 31st October 2000

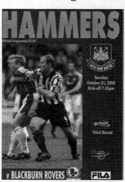

West Ham United 2 (Suker, Di Canio), Blackburn Rovers 0.
Att: 21,863. Referee: A Wiley.
West Ham United: Hislop, Potts, Pearce I, Sinclair, Ferdinand, Pearce S, Lampard, Di Canio, Suker, Carrick, Kanoute (Moncur).
Kelly, Kenna, Curtis, Taylor (Flitcroft), Dailly, Carsley, McAteer, Dunning, Ostenstad, Richards (Dunn), Johnson (Douglas).

Round Four 29th November 2000

West Ham United 1 (Lampard), Sheffield Wednesday 2 (Morrison, Westwood).
Att: 25,853. Referee: P Danson.
West Ham United: Hislop, Song (Suker), Winterburn, Stimac, Ferdinand, Pearce S, Lampard, Di Canio, Sinclair, Carrick, Kanoute.
Sheffield Wednesday: Pressman, Haslam, Geary, Lescott, Westwood, Walker, Crane, Sibon (Booth), Ekoku, Morrison, Quinn.

2001/02

Round Two 11th September 2001

Reading 0, West Ham United 0. West Ham United lost 5-6 on penalties, a.e.t.
Att: 21,173. Referee: W Jordan.
Reading: Whitehead, Murty, Robinson, Whitbread, Williams (Henderson), Parkinson, Igoe, Harper, Cureton (Viveash), Butler (Rougier), Smith.
West Ham United: Hislop, Schemmell, Minto, Hutchison, Song, Dailly, Moncur (Courtois), Todorov (Garcia), Sinclair, Defoe, Carrick.

2002/03

Round Two 1st October 2002

Chesterfield 1 (Brandon), West Ham United 1 (Defoe). West Ham United won 5-4 on penalties, a.e.t. Att: 7,102. Referee: A Hall.
Chesterfield: Muggleton, Davies, Rushbury (Edwards), Dawson, Blatherwick, Howson, Booty (Brandon), Hudson, Allott, Reeves (Burt), Ebdon.
West Ham United: James, Schemell, Minto, Lomas, Repka, Breen, Sinclair, Cole, Defoe, Di Canio, Carrick.

Round Three 6th November 2002

West Ham United 0, Oldham Athletic 1 (Corazzin). Att: 21,919. Referee: U Rennie.
West Ham United: James, Dailly, Minto (Schemmel), Lomas, Pearce, Breen (Winterburn), Camara, Cole, Defoe, Cisse (Garcia), Carrick.
Oldham Athletic: Pogliacomi, Low, Eyres, Beharral, Hall, Hill, Murray, Armstrong, Andrews (Killen), Corazzin, Eyre.

2003/04

Round One 13th August 2003

West Ham United 3 (Defoe, Connolly 2), Rushden & Diamonds 1 (Lowe). Att: 13,715. Referee: M Cowburn.
West Ham United: James, Ferdinand (Garcia), Brevett, Sofiane (Byrne), Repka, Dailly, Noble, Lee, Connolly, Defoe, Etherington. Rushden & Diamonds: Turley, Bignot, Underwood, Bell, Hunter (Dempster), Edwards, Hall, Mills (Gray), Jack (Darby), Lowe, Burgess.

The Hammers started brightly and quickly took a two-goal lead.
After 9 minutes David Connolly chipped the ball on to the crossbar and Jermain Defoe slammed home the rebound. Five minutes later Connolly beat two defenders and planted a low shot into the far corner. After half an hour Christian Dailly gave away a free kick and Lowe fired an unstoppable shot into the top corner to bring the Diamonds back into the game. After 78 minutes man-of-the-match Connolly followed up on Defoe's shot to score Hammers third. Rushden played some good football but could not contain the front two of Connolly and Defoe who were sharp and lively throughout.

Round Two 23rd September 2003

Cardiff, City 2 (Earnshaw 2), West Ham United 3 (Defoe 3). Att: 10,724. Referee: A D'Urso. Cardiff City: Margetson, Weston, Barber, Boland, Gabbidon, Vidmar, Bowen (Campbell), Kavanagh, Earnshaw, Thorne (Gordon), Bonner.

West Ham United: James, Ferdinand, Quinn, Pearce, Repka, Dailly, Horlock, Mellor (Garcia), Connolly, Defoe, Etherington.

In the early stages City threatened to walk away with the tie as Earnshaw scored twice. In the 11th minute Bowen sent in a cross which Earnshaw side-footed home and the striker followed up on this after 24 minutes when he curled a 24-yarder inside the left hand post. After this West Ham showed spirit and character to fight back with a stunning hat-trick from Jermain Defoe.
Just before the interval Vidmar challenged Connolly unfairly in the area and from the penalty spot Defoe drilled his shot into the corner. On 63 minutes the striker was again on hand to unleash a 20 yarder for the equaliser. Defoe completed his hat-trick two minutes from the end after Connolly laid off a pass to him and he thundered in a low shot from 20 yards.

Round Three 29th October 2003

Tottenham Hotspur 1 (Zamora), West Ham United 0. Att: 36,053. Referee: G Poll. Tottenham Hotspur: Keller, Carr, Ziegle (Blondel), Gardner, Doherty, King, Konchesky, Dalmat (Mabizela), Keane, Zamora, Ricketts (Postiga).
West Ham United: James, Stockdale (Ferdinand), Quinn, Horlock (Mellor), Kilgallon, Dailly, Carrick, Lee (Garcia), Hutchison, Defoe, Etherington.

2004/05

Round One 24th August 2004

West Ham United 2 (Harewood 2), Southend United 0. Att: 16,910. Referee: P Armstrong.
West Ham United: Walker, McClenahan, Repka, Ward, Brevett, Chadwick (Noble), Nowland, Reo-Coker, Cohen, Harewood, Rebrov (Sheringham).
Southend United: Griemink, Jupp, Barrett, Edwards, Nicolau, Pettefer, Mahert, Bentley, Gower, Broughton (Bramble), Dudfield (Gray).

Round Two 21st September 2004

West Ham United 3 (Zamora 2, Rebrov), Notts County 2 (Wilson, Richardson). Att: 11,111. Referee: I Williamson.
West Ham United: Walker, Mullins, Brevett, Lomas, MacKay, Repka (Melville), Rebrov, Reo-Coker, Etherington (Cohen).
Notts County: Deeney, Wilson, Ullathorne (Oakes), Richardson, Whitlow, Edwards (Williams), Pipe, Bolland, Scully, Hurst, Gill.

Round Three 27th October 2004

Chelsea 1 (Kezman), West Ham United 0 Att: 41,774. Referee: A D'Urso.
Chelsea: Cudicini, Ferreira, Gallas, Carvalho, Babayaro, Parker (Duff), Cole (Lampard), Geremi, Tiago, Robben (Gudjohnsen), Kezman.
West Ham United: Walker, Mullins, Repka, Ferdinand, Brevett, Etherington (Noble), Lomas, Nowland (Hutchison), Reo-Coker, Zamora (Rebrov), Harewood.

2005/06

Round Two 20th September 2005

Sheffield Wednesday 2 (Coughlan, Graham), West Ham United 4 (Zamora 2, Dailly, Bellion). Att: 14,976. Referee: S Tanner.
Sheffield Wednesday: Lucas, Ross, Coughlan, Wood, Bullen, McGovern (Hills), Whelan (O'Brien), Rocastle, Brunt, Corr (Peacock), Graham.
West Ham United: Hislop, Repka (Stokes), Cohen, Ward, Collins, Dailly, Williams (Ephraim), Newton, Noble, Zamora, Harewood (Bellion).

West Ham made the best possible start taking the lead inside two minutes. A Gavin Williams through-ball found Zamora who made no mistake in firing past the keeper. This led to a period of dominance for the Hammers as Marlon Harewood went close on a couple of occasions.

After the interval a corner from Newton was headed home by Dailly to spark the Hammers fans into full voice. On 62 minutes the tie was almost killed off when a poor clearance came to Bobby Zamora, who sent a volley screaming into the far corner. With a quarter of an hour to go, Wednesday got a goal back when Coughlan headed home a corner from Brunt. Three minutes later Graham curled a low effort past Hislop to make it 3-2.

Hillsborough was now sensing a thrilling comeback as Graham again went close with a shot over the crossbar. However with 6 minutes remaining the Hammers scored a fourth when debutant David Bellion fired low past Lucas.

Round Three 26th October 2005

Bolton Wanderers 1 (Borgetti), West Ham United 0. Att: 10,927. Referee: A Marriner.
Bolton Wanderers: Walker, Ben Haim, Jaidy, O'Brien, Gardner, Diagne-Faye (Djetou), Fernandes (N'Gotty), Nolan, Fadiga, Giannakopoulos (Pedersen), Borgetti.
West Ham United: Hislop, Repka, Collins, Ward, Konchesky, Dailly, Mullins, Clarke (Newton), Bellion, Sheringham (Aliadiere), Harewood (Fletcher).

2006/07

Round Three 24th October 2006
Chesterfield 2 (Larkin, Folan), West Ham United 1 (Harewood).
Att: 7,787. Referee: L Probert.
Chesterfield: Roche, Bailey (Lowry), Hazell, Downes, O'Hare, Hall, Niven, Allott, Hurst, Folan, Larkin (Allison).
West Ham United: Green, Pantsill, Gabbidon, Ferdinand, McCartney (Konchesky), Reo-Coker, Mullins, Dailly, Reid (Etherington), Harewood (Sheringham), Zamora.

2007/08

Round Two 28th August 2007

Bristol Rovers 1 (Williams), West Ham United 2 (Bellamy 2).
Att: 10,831. Referee: M Jones.
Bristol Rovers: Phillips, Lescott, Carruthers, Campbell, Anthony, Elliott, Pipe, Disley (Igoe), Walker, Lambert (Williams), Jacobson (Haldane).
West Ham United: Wright, Neill, Ferdinand, Gabbidon, McCartney (Collins), Dyer (Noble), Mullins, Bowyer, Boa Morte, Zamora, Bellamy (Cole).

Round Three 26th September 2007

West Ham United 1 (Ashton), Plymouth Argyle 0.
Att: 25,774.
Referee: P Dowd.
West Ham United: Wright, Neill, Collins, Gabbidon, McCartney, Ljunberg (Bowyer), Mullins, Parker (Noble), Boa Morte, Ashton, Cole (Reid).
Plymouth Argyle: McCormick, Connolly, Sawyer (Chadwick), Buzsaky, Timar, Seip, Norris, Nalis, Ebanks-Blake (Fallon), Hayles, Halmosi.

Round Four 30th October 2007

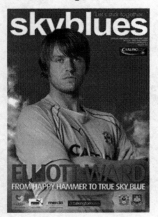

Coventry City 1 (Tabb), West Ham United 2 (Cole, Boa Morte).
Att: 23,968.
Referee: R Styles.
Coventry City: Marshall, McNamee, Hall, Doyle, Turner, De, Zeeuw, Osbourne, Gray (Simpson), Best (Kyle), Mifsud, Tabb.
West Ham United: Wright, Neill, Ferdinand (Gabbidon), Upson, McCartney, Bowyer, Mullins (Spector), Noble (Pantsill), Etherington, Boa Morte, Cole.

Quarter-final 12th December 2007

West Ham United 1 (Cole), Everton 2 (Osman, Yakubu).
Att: 28,777.
Referee: M Halsey.
West Ham United: Green, Neill, Upson, Gabbidon, McCartney, Ljunberg, Mullins, Parker, Boa Morte (Reid), Ashton, Cole (Pantsil).
Everton: Howard, Neville, Yobo, Jagielka, Lescott, Osman, Pienaar, Carsley, Arteta, Cahill, Yakubu.

2008/09

Round Two 27th August 2008

West Ham United 4 (Bowyer, Cole, Hines, Reid), Macclesfield Town 1 (Evans).
Att: 10,055.
Referee: C Penton.
West Ham United: Green, Behrami (Hines), Davenport, Upson, McCartney (Reid), Faubert, Mullins, Bowyer, Boa Morte, Sears (Cole), Ashton.
Macclesfield Town: Brian, Brisley, Hessey, Walker, Reid, Tolley, Bell, Thomas (Yeo), Deen, Evans (Rooney), Green (Hadfield).

The Boleyn Ground was stunned after five minutes as the League Two side took the lead when Evans headed home following a corner. For the Hammers, Dean Ashton was looking lively and his snap shot was well saved by Brian. Just before half-time Ashton was again unlucky as he skipped by two defenders and his curling shot clipped the crossbar.

There was continuous pressure in the second half and on 74 minutes the equaliser came when Julian Faubert crossed to Lee Bowyer who headed home. In the closing stages the visiting full back Reid was sent off for gaining two yellow cards.

The tie went into extra-time and after ten minutes Carlton Cole scored following a header from Ashton. The Hammers were now in control and Zavon Hines added a third before Kyle Reid scored a fourth with a neat shot.

Round Three 23rd September 2008

Watford 1 (Mullins (og)), West Ham United 0.
Att: 12,914. Referee: P Walton.
Watford: Loach, Mariappa, Parkes, Bromby, Demerit, Williamson (Bennett), Ainsworth, Bangura, Jenkins, Smith (Harley), Hoskins (Young).
West Ham United: Lastuvka, Neill, Lopez, Upson, Etherington, Boa Morte (Parker), Noble, Mullins, Faubert, Di Michele (Reid), Sears.

2009/10

Round Two 25th August 2009

West Ham United 3 (Stanislas 2, Hines), Millwall 1 (Harris).
Att: 24,492. Referee: P Taylor.
West Ham United: Green, Faubert, Tomkins, Gabbidon, Spector, Kovac (Nouble), Parker, Collison, Payne (Hines), Stanislas, Cole (Upson).
Millwall: Forde, Dunne, Smith, Frampton, Barron, Hackett, Fuseini, Laird, Martin (Price), Harris (Grimes), Alexander (Bolder).

These two fierce rivals met in a keenly fought affair played in a tense atmosphere as rival fans clashed off the pitch. On 24 minutes the Lions top scorer Harris gave them the lead as he latched onto Barron's throw and drove a shot past Green. The arrival of Hines who came on as a substitute saw an increase in attacking play from West Ham. He exchanged passes with Collison who crashed a shot against the inside of the post. The Hammers committed more and more men forward and with just 3 minutes remaining Faubert found the unmarked Stanislas who gleefully converted.

The tie went into extra time and after 7 minutes a cross from Hines was handled in the area by Frampton and Stanislas scored from the spot. Five minutes later Hines raced into the box and shot powerfully past Forde. The fans were ecstatic as a mini pitch invasion followed.

Round Three 22nd September 2009

Bolton Wanderers 3 (Davies, Cahill, Elmander), West Ham United 1 (Ilunga)
Att: 8,050. Referee: H Webb.
Bolton Wanderers: Jaaskelainen, Ricketts, Cahill, Knight, Samuel, Muamba, McCann (Cohen), Taylor, Gardner (Lee), Davies, Klasnic (Elmander).
West Ham United: Green, Spector, Da Costa (N'Gala), Tomkins, Ilunga, Noble, Parker, Kovac, Dyer (Cole), Hines (Faubert), Diamanti.

2010/11

Round Two 24th August 2010

West Ham United 1 (Parker), Oxford United 0.
Att: 20,902.
Referee: J Linington.
West Ham United: Stech, Faubert, Ben Haim, Tomkins, Spector, Barrera, Noble, Parker, Stanislas (Cole), Sears (McCarthy), Piquionne.
Oxford United: Clarke, Purkiss, Worley, Wright, Tonkin, Potter (Green), Bulman (Baker), Heslop, Hall, Constable, Cole (Clist).

Round Three 21st September 2010

Sunderland 1 (Gyan), West Ham United 2 (Piquionne, Obinna).
Att: 21,907.
Referee: H Webb.
Sunderland: Mignolet, Bardsley, Onuoha, Ferdinand (Da Silva), Richardson, Almuhamady, Henderson (Zenden), Riveros, Welbeck, Bent, Guyan (Malbranque).
West Ham United: Stech, Faubert, Da Costa, Tomkins, Ben Haim, Barrera (Noble), Parker, Kovac, Boa Morte, Piquionne (Cole), Obinna (Dyer).

Round Four 27th October 2010

West Ham United 3 (Parker, Da Costa, Obinna), Stoke City 1 (Jones).
Att: 25,304. Referee: H Webb.
West Ham United: Stech, Faubert, Da Costa, Tomkins, Ben Haim, Barrera, Kovac (Obinna), Parker, Boa Morte (Behrami), Cole, McCarthy (Noble).
Stoke City: Begovic, Wilkinson, Huth Shawcross, Higginbotham, Pennant (Pugh), Whelan, Whitbread, Tuncay (Delap), Jones (Gudjohnsen), Walters.

Quarter-final 30th November 2010

West Ham United 4 (Spector 2, Cole 2), Manchester United 0.
Att: 33,551. Referee: M Clattenberg.
West Ham United: Green, Faubert, Tomkins (Reid), Upson, Ben Haim, Barrera (Hines), Kovac, Spector, Boa Morte, Cole (Stanislas), Obinna.
Manchester United: Kuszczak, O'Shea, Smalling, Evans (Brown), Da Silva F (Da Silva R), Obertan, Fletcher, Anderson, Giggs, Hernandez, Bebe (Macheda).

In sub-zero temperatures at a snow bound Upton Park the fans were warmed up with a brilliant display that knocked out the Carling Cup holders.

On 7 minutes there was an outstanding save from Robert Green as he dived to push Obertans shot onto the post. Nine minutes later West Ham thought they had taken the lead: Obinna hit a shot but on its way it clipped Spector before hitting the net; since Spector was in an offside position the goal was disallowed. On 22 minutes Obinna clipped a cross into the area and Spector dived to send a header beyond Kuszczak.

After 37 minutes Spector scored again after Obinna scuffed his shot; the American latched on to a loose ball before firing home

from close range. Eleven minutes into the second half Obinna found Cole with a cross and the big forward headed powerfully into the net. Ten minutes later the outstanding Obinna slid a ball inside for Cole who held off his marker before slamming a shot past the advancing keeper.

It was a superb all round performance by the team and gave them confidence in their fight against relegation from the Premier League.

Semi-final first leg 11th January 2011

West Ham United 2 (Noble , Cole), Birmingham City 1 (Ridgewell).
Att 34,754.
Referee: P Dowd.
West Ham United: Green, Faubert, Tomkins, Reid, Upson, Spector, Sears (Hines), Noble (Kovac) Parker, Obinna, Piquionne (Cole).
Birmingham City: Foster, Carr, Dann (Murphy), Johnson, Ridgewell, Larsson (Zigic), Gardner, Hleb (Beausejour), Ferguson, Fahey, Jerome.

Semi-final second leg 26th January 2011
Birmingham City 3 (Bowyer, Johnson, Gardner), West Ham United 1 (Cole).
Att: 27,519.
Referee: H Webb.
Birmingham City: Foster, Carr, Johnson, Jiranek ,Ridgewell, Larsson (Murphy), Ferguson,Bowyer,Gardner (Beausejoor), Derbyshire (Zigic), Jerome.
West Ham United: Green, Faubert, Tomkins, Upson, Bridge, Noble, Parker, Spector (McCarthy), Hines (Dyer), Cole, Boa Morte (O'Neil).

APPENDIX 1: STATISTICS

Complete Playing Record:

	P	W	D	L	F	A
Home	104	72	16	16	246	90
Away	90	31	21	38	121	143
Neutral	4	0	2	2	4	6
Total	198	103	39	56	371	239

Biggest Wins

Home: 10-0 v Bury, 25th October 1983
Away: 5-1 v Cardiff City, 25th February 1966
Away: 5-1 v Walsall, 13th September 1967

Biggest Defeats

Home: 2-5 v Barnsley, 6th October 1987
Away: 0-5 v Nottm Forest, 30th August 1977
Away: 0-5 v Tottenham Hotspur, 2nd February 1987

Largest Attendances

Home: 40,878 v Liverpool, 27th October 1971
Away: 49,125 v Tottenham Hotspur, 12th November 1975
Neutral: (Wembley) 100,000 v Liverpool, 14th March 1981

Smallest Attendances

Home: 6,891 v Crewe Alexandra, 23rd September 1992
Away: 3,849 v Barnet, 18th September 1996

Hat Tricks

Johnny Byrne v Plymouth Argyle, home, 26th September 1962
Johnny Byrne v Workington, home, 16th December 1963
John Sissons v Leeds United, home, 7th November 1966
Geoff Hurst v Leeds United, home, 7th November 1966
Geoff Hurst v Bolton Wanderers, home, 4th September 1968
Bryan Robson v Sheffield United, home, 17th November 1971
Bobby Gould v Tranmere Rovers, home, 18th September 1974
Billy Lansdowne v Southend United, home, 8th October 1979
Francois Van der Elst v Notts County, away, 7th December 1982
Tony Cottee v Preston North End, home, 7th October 1986
Frank Lampard v Walsall, home, 19th November 1987
Jermain Defoe v Cardiff City, away, 23rd September 2003

Four Goals

Geoff Hurst v Bolton Wanderers, home, 11th October 1967
Tony Cottee v Bury, home, 25th October 1983

Opposition Hat Tricks

Jeff Astle, West Bromwich Albion, 18th January 1967
Clive Allen, Tottenham Hotspur, 2nd February 1987

Top Goalscorers

Geoff Hurst	43
Tony Cottee	18

With another 6 goals scored for Stoke City, Geoff Hurst is joint holder with Ian Rush of the record for most goals scored in the League Cup, 49.

In the 1965/66 tournament, Hurst scored 11 times in 10 games.

Most Appearances

Alvin Martin	71
Billy Bonds	67

Dismissals

West Ham:

Billy Bonds v Hull City, 9th September 1970
Paul Allen v West Bromwich Albion, 1st
December 1981
Julian Dicks v Wimbledon, 22nd November
1989
Martin Allen v Derby County, 17th January
1990
Victor Obinna v Birmingham City, 11th
January 2011

Opposition:

Tony Brown, West Bromwich Albion, 1st
December 1981
Izak Reid, Macclesfield Town, 27th August
2008

Most Substitutions

Carlton Cole   6
Mark Noble   6

Miscellaneous

West Ham have used a total of 277 players in
the League Cup and made 161 substitutions.

APPENDIX 2: LEAGUE CUP APPEARANCES AND GOALS

Player	Apps	Goals	Player	Apps	Goals
Abou Samassi	2 + 1	1	Camara Titi	1	
Aliadiere Jeremie	0 + 1		Carrick Michael	8	
Allen Clive	2		Cartwright John	1	
Allen Martin	15 + 3	5	Chadwick Luke	1	
Allen Paul	20 + 4	2	Chapman Lee	4 + 1	2
Ashton Dean	3	1	Charles Gary	1	
Ayris John	6 + 1	1	Charles John	19	1
Banton Dale	1		Cisse Edouard	1	
Barnes Bobby	2 + 2		Clark Sandy	7	3
Barrera Pablo	4		Clarke Clive	1	
Behrami Valon	1 + 1		Cohen Chris	2 + 1	
Bellamy Craig	1	2	Cole Carlton	7 + 6	7
Bellion David	1 + 1	1	Cole Joe	6 + 1	1
Ben Haim Tal	4		Coleman Keith	6	
Bennett Peter	3		Collins James	3 + 1	
Berkovic Eyal	6		Collison Jack	1	
Best Clyde	20	8	Connolly David	2	2
Bickles Dave	1		Cottee Tony	27	18
Bilic Slaven	5	1	Courtois Laurent	0 + 1	
Bishop Ian	21 + 1	1	Cowie George	1	
Boa Morte Louis	10	1	Crawford Ian	1	2
Boere Jeroen	1 + 1	1	Cross David	24	12
Bond John	13	1	Cross Roger	1	
Bonds Billy	65 + 2	6	Curbishley Alan	3	
Bovington Eddie	18	1	Cushley John	4	
Bowen Mark	3		Da Costa Manuel	3	1
Bowyer Lee	3 + 1	1	Dailly Christian	8	1
Boyce Ronnie	23	2	Davenport Calum	1	
Brabrook Peter	23	6	Day Mervyn	14	
Brady Liam	14 + 3		Dear Brian	3	
Breacker Tim	20 + 1		Defoe Jermain	6+1	6
Breen Gary	2		Devonshire Alan	45 + 3	2
Brevett Rufus	4		Diamanti Alessandro	1	
Bridge Wayne	1		Di Canio Paolo	7	1
Britt Martin	6	1	Dick John	4	2
Brooking Trevor	55	8	Dickens Alan	14 + 3	3
Brown Ken	28		Dickie Alan	2	
Brown Kenny	2 + 1		Dicks Julian	30	8
Brush Paul	12 + 1		Di Michele David	1	
Burkett Jack	17		Dolan Eamonn	4	
Burnett Dennis	10	2	Dowie Iain	10 + 1	2
Burrows David	3	1	Dumitrescu Ilie	2 + 1	
Butler Peter	4		Dunmore Dave	2	1
Byrne Johnny	19	15	Dyer Keiron	2 + 2	
Byrne Shaun	0 + 1		Ephraim Hogan	0 + 1	

Player	Apps	Goals	Player	Apps	Goals
Etherington Mattie	7 + 1		Kitchener Bill	1	
Eustace Peter	2 + 1	1	Kitson Paul	2 + 2	1
Fashanu Justin	0 + 1		Konchesky Paul	1 + 1	
Faubert Julian	9 + 1		Kovac Radoslav	5 + 1	
Ferdinand Anton	6 + 1		Lampard Frank	54	1
Ferdinand Rio	11 + 1		Lampard Frank jnr	14 + 1	8
Ferguson Bobby	19		Lansdowne Billy	4 + 1	3
Fletcher Carl	0 + 1		Lastuvka Jan	1	
Foe Marc-Vivien	3		Lazaridis Stan	6 + 1	
Forrest Craig	3		Lee Robert	2	
Foster Colin	5		Leslie Lawrie	3	
Gabbidon Danny	5 + 1		Lindsay Jimmy	2	
Gale Tony	28 + 2	1	Ljunberg Freddie	2	
Gallager Joe	1		Lock Kevin	13	
Garcia Richard	0 + 5		Lomas Steve	13	2
Goddard Paul	26	12	Lopez Walter	1	
Gordon Dale	1		Lyall John	2	
Gould Bobby	2	3	MacDougall Ted	1	1
Greaves Jimmy	1		Mackay Malky	1	
Green Robert	8		Malcolm Andy	2	
Green Bill	3		Margas Javier	2	
Grice Mike	1		Marsh Mike	6	
Grotier Peter	4		Martin Alvin	71	6
Harewood Marlon	6	3	Mautone Steve	2	
Hartson John	6	6	McAlister Tom	7	
Hilton Paul	6 + 2		McAvennie Frank	11 + 2	2
Hines Zavon	2 + 4	2	McCarthy Benni	1 + 2	
Hislop Shaka	12		McCartney George	6	
Holland Pat	22 + 3	3	McClenahan Trent	1	
Holmes Matt	4		McDowell John	21	1
Horlock Kevin	2		McGiven Mick	2	
Howe Bobby	2 + 2		McKnight Alan	6	
Hughes Michael	7		McQueen Tommy	2+ 3	
Hurst Geoff	47	43	Mellor Neil	1 + 1	
Hutchison Don	5 + 1	2	Melville Andy	0 + 1	
Ilunga Herita	1	1	Miklosko Ludek	25	
Impey Andy	4		Milne Ralph	0 + 1	
Ince Paul	9	3	Minto Scott	4	
James David	5		Moncur John	13 + 1	2
Jennings Billy	3 + 2		Moore Bobby	49	3
Jones Steve	0 + 1		Morgan Nicky	1	
Kanoute Fredi	3		Morley Trevor	10 + 1	5
Keen Kevin	21 + 1	5	Mullins Hayden	10	
Keller Marc	4 + 1	1	Musgrove Malcolm	5	3
Kelly David	11 + 3	5	Neighbour Jimmy	11 + 1	1
Kilgallon Matt	1		Neil Lucas	5	
Kirkup Joe	7		Newton Shaun	1 + 1	

Player	Apps	Goals	Player	Apps	Goals
N'Gala Bondz	0 + 1		Sinclair Trevor	9 + 1	
Noble David	1		Sissons John	21	5
Noble Mark	7 + 6	1	Slater Robbie	3	
Nouble Frank	0 + 1		Slater Stuart	16 + 1	2
Nowland Adam	2		Small Mike	4 + 1	4
Obinna Victor	3 + 1	2	Smith Mark	1	
Omoyinmi Manny	0 + 1		Sofiane Youseff	1	
O'Neil Gary	0 + 1		Song Rigobert	2	
Orhan Yilmaz	1		Spector Jonathan	6 + 1	2
Orr Neil	14 + 4	1	Standen Jim	23	
Paddon Graham	11	2	Stanislas Junior	2 + 1	2
Pantsill John	1 + 2		Stech Marek	3	
Parker Scott	9 + 1	2	Stephenson Alan	6	
Parkes Phil	52		Stewart Ray	44	14
Parris George	27 + 3	1	Stimac Igor	5	
Payne Josh	1		Stockdale Robbie	1	
Pearce Ian	8		Stokes Tony	0 + 1	
Pearce Stuart	4		Strodder Gary	8	
Pearson Stuart	3 + 2	1	Suker Davor	1 + 1	1
Peters Martin	31	10	Swindlehurst David	5	1
Pike Geoff	38 + 1	3	Taylor Alan	8	2
Piquionne Freddie	3	1	Taylor Tommy	26	
Porfirio Hugo	2	1	Thomas Mitchell	5	
Potts Steve	39 + 3		Todorov Svetoslav	1	
Quinn Jimmy	3	1	Tomkins James	8	
Quinn Wayne	2		Tyler Dudley	3	
Radford John	1		Unsworth David	5	
Raducioiu Florin	1	1	Upson Matthew	7 + 1	
Rebrov Sergei	2 + 1	1	Van Der Elst Francois	5 + 1	3
Redknapp Harry	17 + 1	1	Walford Steve	16 + 1	2
Reid Kyle	1 + 4	1	Walker James	3	
Reid Winston	1 + 1		Wanchope Paulo	2	
Reo-Coker Nigel	4		Ward Elliott	3	
Repka Tomas	8		Ward Mark	20 + 1	2
Rhodes Brian	3		Whitbread Adrian	2 + 1	
Rieper Marc	6 + 1		Whitton Steve	6	2
Robson Bryan	15	6	Williams Gavin	1	
Robson Keith	7	1	Williamson Danny	0 + 2	
Robson Mark	2		Winterburn Nigel	3 + 1	
Robson Stewart	8	1	Woodley Derek	1	
Rosenior Leroy	7	2	Woosnam Phil	4	1
Rowland Keith	3 + 2		Wright Ian	2	
Ruddock Neil	3 + 1		Wright Richard	3	
Rush Matthew	4		Zamora Bobby	5	4
Schemmel Seb	2 + 1				
Scott Tony	7	3	Own Goals		6
Sealey Alan	6	1	Totals	2178	371
Sears Freddie	4		Substitutes	161	
Sheringham Teddy	1 + 2				

APPENDIX 3: THE OMOYINMI AFFAIR

Quarter-final 15th December 1999
West Ham United 2 (Lampard, Di Canio),
Aston Villa 2 (Taylor, Dublin), a.e.t.
West Ham won 5-4 on penalties.
Att: 23,974. Referee: A Lodge
West Ham United: Hislop, Ferdinand,
Ruddock, Margas, Sinclair, Lampard,
Lomas, Keller, Cole (Kitson) Di Canio,
Wanchope (Omoyinmi).
Aston Villa: James, Ehiogu, Southgate, Barry,
Watson, Taylor, Merson (Vassell), Boating,
Wright, Dublin, Joachim (Stone).

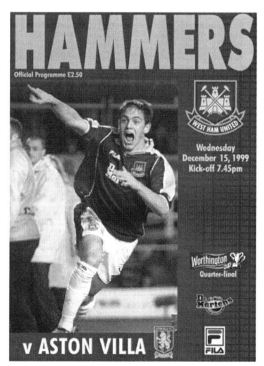

When Dublin scored for the Villa in the 89th minute it seemed that the Hammers were going out of the competition. However in the last minute Wright challenged Kitson in the area to concede a penalty, and up stepped Di Canio to score the equaliser.

The game went into extra time and with six minutes remaining Omoyinmi came on as a substitute to replace Wanchope. In those six minutes he only touched the ball twice and his involvement in the game was insignificant. However it turned out later that his inclusion was to have serious consequences for the club and their supporters.

The tie was then to be decided on penalties and when Southgate missed with the last kick it gave West Ham a 5-4 win. The team celebrated with their ecstatic fans as they looked forward to facing Leicester City in the semi-finals.

The following day brought bewilderment and heartache as it was discovered that Omoyinmi was not eligible to play as he had been on loan to Gillingham and had played for them in an earlier League Cup tie with Bolton Wanderers.

An official statement was then issued by the club an extract of which read:

"When the player returned from his loan period West Ham believed that he had not played for Gillingham in the Worthington Cup. West Ham now acknowledge that this was not the case but wishes to emphasise that the club acted in good faith. Omoyinmi appeared for six minutes only and had no influence on the result of the tie.
West Ham firmly believe that the tie was won fairly, that the result should stand and that no further action is necessary."

Of course the reaction from Aston Villa was in contrast. The Villa chairman Doug Ellis complained to the Football League while the Villa secretary Steve Stride said "We are treating this as a serious breach of the rules, and trust the outcome will reflect the seriousness of the matter."

The Football league later ruled that the tie should be replayed and the result and match details erased from the records. In the replay West Ham lost 1-3 after extra time after being in the lead until 10 minutes from the end.

The repercussions of the event followed as the West Ham secretary Graham Mackrell and Football secretary Alison O'Dowd both resigned and left the club. Omoyinmi was immediately sent out on loan to Scunthorpe and never played for the club again.

Talking later, manager Harry Redknapp expressed his surprise and disappointment that the player had not said something at the time.

APPENDIX 4: THE FOOTBALL LEAGUE CUP

The Football League Cup began in 1960/61 and has been a sponsored competition since 1981/82:

1981/82 to 1985/86	The Milk Cup
1986/87 to 1989/90	The Littlewoods Challenge Cup
1990/91 & 1991/92	The Rumbelows League Cup
1992/93 to 1997/98	The Coca Cola Cup
1998/99 to 2002/03	The Worthington Cup
2003/04 onwards	The Carling Cup

The Football League originally proposed the League Cup as part of a scheme to reduce the number of clubs in each division and consequently the number of games played each season. However, the reduction in numbers was not agreed to by the League's member clubs, so the ties had to be squeezed into the existing fixture list.

The new competition soon attracted a good deal of criticism. The Wolves chairman thought it "not in the best interests of the game". The Times' correspondent stated "our game is now further to be saddled by a pointless, prosaic, parochial new tournament". Opposition to the tournament has a familiar ring even today, being based largely on the assumption that clubs already had too many games to play in League, FA Cup and Europe. However, the Football League saw the competition as a useful money-spinner for the smaller clubs.

Ties were intended to be played mid-week under floodlights. However, some 3pm kick-offs were needed since not all clubs had floodlights in 1960. Weeks in the season are now set aside for ties, but the first season was not organised this way; with a number of clubs having byes in round one, some second round ties were played before first round games.

Entry to the competition was not mandatory for League clubs until 1971/72. 1960/61 saw 87 entrants, the missing clubs being Arsenal, Sheffield Wednesday, Tottenham Hotspur, West Bromwich Albion and Wolves. These clubs had filled four of the top five places in the First Division of 1959/60.

Entries in subsequent years were as follows:

1961/62	82
1962/63	80
1963/64	82
1964/65	82
1965/66	83
1966/67	90
1967/68	90
1968/69	91

The increase in the number of clubs entering in 1966/67 reflected the decision to play the final at Wembley and also to grant entry to winner to the European Inter-Cities Fairs Cup (later the UEFA Cup). 1969/70 was the first season when all 92 clubs entered, though Everton missed the 1970/71 season. After entry became compulsory in 1971/72, Luton Town were disqualified in 1986/87 because of the club's ban on away supporters entering their ground.

The first games took place under floodlights on 26th September 1960. Bristol Rovers beat Fulham 2-1 and West Ham beat Charlton Athletic 3-1. The first goal in the competition was scored by Maurice Cook, Fulham's centre forward, in the 9th minute.

The first final was between Aston Villa (who finished 9th in the First Division) and Rotherham United (15th in the Second). The two-legged final was held over until the start of the next season. Rotherham won 2-0 at home. The second leg, played in heavy rain, saw Villa leading 2-0 after 90 minutes. Extra time was played, during which Peter McParland scored the deciding goal for Villa.

The next season saw Norwich City of the Second Division playing Rochdale of the Fourth, after both clubs had beaten First Division opponents in the semi-finals. Rochdale remain the only club from the lowest of the four divisions to have played in the final. Norwich built up a commanding lead in the away leg of the final so that the second leg was something of a formality.

Aston Villa reached their second final in 1963. The first "all First Division" final saw Birmingham City perform well enough at home to win the first major trophy in their history. The next season produced a win for Leicester City over Stoke City, some reward for them perhaps after a sequence of losing Wembley finals in the FA Cup.

Leicester reached the final again the following year, losing to Chelsea. Leicester thus became the first in the list of clubs who have defended the League Cup well enough to reach the next final, only to lose. The other clubs with this sad record are West Bromwich Albion, Nottingham Forest, Arsenal and Luton Town.

The last two-legged final in 1966 was the only occasion on which a club overcame a first leg deficit to win the trophy. West Ham had a 2-1 lead after the first leg at home, but West Bromwich played well in the second leg to win 5-3 on aggregate.

The first Wembley final in 1967 produced a major upset. West Bromwich were hot favourites to retain the trophy against Third Division Queen's Park Rangers. At half time, West Bromwich held a 2-0 lead and the game looked to be over. However, a great fightback, with Rodney Marsh prominent, saw the Rangers home by 3 goals to 2. Queen's Park Rangers were denied a place in the Fairs Cup because they were not a First Division club; West Bromwich took their place.

Leeds United and Arsenal fought out a close game in 1968, the winning Leeds goal from Terry Cooper being hotly disputed following a charge on goalkeeper Jim Furnell.

Arsenal returned to Wembley in 1969, only to become the victim of another piece of "giant killing". Swindon Town had beaten two First Division teams to reach the final, but were given little chance against Arsenal. On a poor Wembley pitch the game went to extra time, when two goals for Swindon gave them a deserved victory. Don Rogers had an outstanding game, scoring two of Swindon's goals.

No third division club has won the League Cup since then; indeed the second division can only claim two wins. The 1970s saw five of the leading clubs of the time achieve two wins each; Manchester City, Tottenham Hotspur, Wolves, Aston Villa and Nottingham Forest.

West Bromwich played their third final in 1970. On a muddy pitch, with snow piled up behind the goals, West Bromwich took a five-minute lead against Manchester City through Jeff Astle. There used to be a saying in the FA Cup that the first club to score would win the cup, but this has proved not to be a reliable forecast in League Cup finals. Manchester City fought back to win 2-1 after extra time.

In 1971 it was Aston Villa's turn to play their third final, this time as a third division club. Martin Chivers of Tottenham Hotspur scored the first goal against the run of play and the Spurs went on to win 2-0.

Stoke City achieved their first major cup win in 1972 when they beat Chelsea in the final. They needed two replays and a Gordon Banks penalty save from Geoff Hurst to beat West Ham in the semi-final. George Eastham, by then reaching the veteran stage, scored the winning goal for Stoke in the final.

Tottenham Hotspur became the first club to win the trophy twice. Their opponents in 1973 were Norwich City, so one of the finalists was certain to achieve the honour! A Ralph Coates goal in the 72nd minute was the only one of the game.

1974 saw one of those goalkeeping performances where the natural laws of the universe seem to have been overcome. Gary Pierce in the Wolves goal made outstanding saves from a Manchester City forward line that reads like a "who's who" of British football in the 1970s; Summerbee, Bell, Lee, Law and Marsh. Wolves won 2-1.

1975 was unusual in that no First Division clubs reached the semi-finals. Fourth Division Chester City came within a whisker of beating Aston Villa, then of the Second Division, in the semi-final, but Villa won through to meet Norwich City. Having lost the 1973 final, Norwich had then lost narrowly to Wolves in the 1974 semi-final, so both clubs were regarded as League Cup experts. An interesting twist was that the Villa manager, Ron Saunders, was leading a team out at Wembley for the third successive year; he had been manager of the losing Norwich and Manchester City teams. It was third time lucky for Ron, as Villa won the first all Second Division final with a penalty goal from Ray Graydon after Mel Machin had dived full length to punch away a Chris Nicholl header.

A spectacular overhead kick by Dennis Tueart won an entertaining 1976 final for Manchester City against Newcastle United. 1977 saw Aston Villa back again, once more as a First Division club. A dull 0-0 draw against Everton was followed by another draw in the replay, thanks to a last minute Everton equaliser. The second replay would have been settled by a penalty shoot-out, but this proved unnecessary as Villa won 3-2. Chris Nicholl scored one of the Villa goals with a tremendous long-range drive and the winner from Brian Little came with just two minutes left to play.

1978 saw Nottingham Forest matched with Liverpool. Forest had a sensational season, taking Liverpool's championship the year after they were promoted from the Second Division. Some of the Forest championship team were "cup-tied" and unable to take part in the final. This gave teenage Chris Woods his opportunity in the Forest goal, and he made some good saves to keep the Wembley final to 0-0. The replay saw John Robertson score from the penalty spot after a professional foul by Phil Thompson on John O'Hare, which a TV replay later seemed to show was outside the penalty area. This was enough to win the cup for Forest, who thus became the first club to achieve a League and League Cup double.

Forest became the first club to retain the trophy when they beat Southampton in the 1979, despite falling a goal behind. Their fine run continued to a third final against Wolves in 1980, but a mix-up in defence gave Andy Gray a goal and Wolves the trophy.

If Liverpool were upset by the events of the 1978 final, they put the record straight with an amazing four consecutive wins, a record unlikely to be repeated. None of the wins were easy, all four of the Wembley finals needing extra time. Second Division West Ham took them to a replay in 1981, taking the lead at Villa Park before Liverpool fought back to win 2-1. Tottenham Hotspur took the lead in the 1982 final, the first League Cup sponsored by the Milk Marketing Board. Ronnie Whelan equalised with four minutes remaining and Liverpool scored two more in extra time. Manchester United reached the final for the first time in 1983, scored first through 17 year old Norman Whiteside, but were unable to stop Liverpool winning 2-1 after extra time. Bob Paisley collected the cup in his retirement season.

Liverpool's fourth win was against Everton. The all-Merseyside final was drawn 0-0; a Graham Souness volley in the replay was enough to keep the trophy at Anfield. Liverpool had just one defeat in these four seasons, a second leg semi-final against Burnley.

Norwich City achieved their second win in 1985, against Sunderland. Both finalists had the misfortune to be relegated from the First Division at the end of the season. Chris Woods was now playing for Norwich, and had a penalty to save, but the shot was pulled wide of the goal. A deflected shot was enough to give Norwich their victory.

Only one non-First Division club had reached the quarter-finals in 1985, and this was repeated in 1986 and 1987. Oxford United and Queen's Park Rangers reached the 1986 final. It was Oxford's day, and they won a one-sided final by three goals to none.

The first Littlewoods Cup final in 1987 was a heavyweight affair between Arsenal and Liverpool. Liverpool scored first, but two Charlie Nicholas goals gave Arsenal the trophy.

With twelve minutes remaining of the 1988 final, few would have doubted that Arsenal were going to retain the cup; 2-1 up, and with a penalty awarded in their favour. However, Andy Dibble saved the penalty and Luton scored twice in the last 7 minutes to snatch an amazing victory.

Luton returned to Wembley in 1989, scored first, but lost 3-1 to Nottingham Forest. Forest had also won the Full Members Cup that season, then known as the Simod Cup. Forest were back next season, to face Second Division Oldham Athletic who were having an outstanding season. A single Nigel Jemson goal gave Forest the cup, so equalling Liverpool's (then) record of four wins.

A Second Division club was at Wembley in 1991 for the first Rumbelows Cup final, and this time were successful. Sheffield Wednesday beat Manchester United with a single goal from John Sheriden. Manchester United reached the final again in 1992, where they met Nottingham Forest. A Brian McClair goal enabled United to become the first losing finalists in the League Cup to return in the next season and take the trophy.

1992/93 was the first season of the FA Premier League. At the time of writing, only Premiership clubs have won the League Cup since that season; Manchester United, Liverpool and Chelsea have each won three times.

72

Sheffield Wednesday took an early lead in the 1993 final before Arsenal fought back in the second half to win 2-1. Aston Villa enjoyed an emphatic win over Manchester United in 1994 and two Steve McManaman goals helped Liverpool beat Football League Division One Bolton Wanderers in 1995. Villa won again, 3-0 against Leeds United in 1996.

Leicester City and Middlesbrough were unable to score in the 90 minutes of the 1997 final. Ravanelli scored for Middlesbrough in extra time, then an Emile Heskey goal two minutes from the end of the game earned Leicester a replay at Hillsborough. There was again no score in the first 90 minutes of the replay; a Steve Claridge goal for Leicester in extra-time won them the Cup.

The 1998 final between Chelsea and Division One Middlesbrough was the third consecutive final game with a 0-0 scoreline at the end of normal time. Sinclair and Di Matteo scored for Chelsea in extra-time to win the Cup for the first time since 1965. Leicester City were back at Wembley for the finals of 1999 and 2000. Spurs beat them with a last minute goal from Neilsen in 1999. Division One Tranmere Rovers fought hard in the 2000 final, but had a player sent off as Leicester won 2-1.

A fifth round tie in 1999/2000 between West Ham and Aston Villa was seemingly won by the Hammers in a penalty shoot out when Gareth Southgate missed for Villa. However, when the Football League checked the team sheets it noticed that West Ham had used Manny Omoyinmi as a substitute. Unfortunately he had also played for Gillingham in the competition whilst on loan earlier in the seaon. There was the possibility of disqualification for West Ham, but the League decided the game should be played again. Villa won the re-arranged game 3-1.

Another Division One club, Birmingham City, reached the first final to be played at the Millennium Stadium, Cardiff. A dramatic last minute penalty, converted by Darren Purse, took the game with Liverpool to extra-time, followed by the first penalty shoot-out in a final. Westerveld saved Andrew Johnson's effort to win the Cup for Liverpool by 5 penalties to 4.

The Millennium Stadium roof was closed for the 2002 final between Blackburn Rovers and Tottenham Hotspur. Goals from Jansen and Andy Cole won a close-fought game to give Rovers their first League Cup triumph. Liverpool resumed their outstanding League Cup form in 2003 with a 2-0 win over Manchester United. Middlesbrough won a final at the third time of trying in 2004. They were 2-0 up after 7 minutes; Bolton scored through Davies in the 21st minute, but there were no more goals.

Liverpool were back again in 2005, with the first 'first minute' goal in the finals, thanks to Riise. An own goal from Gerrard for Chelsea took the game to extra-time. Two goals in five minutes tipped the game Chelsea's way; Nunez scored for Liverpool just a minute later but they could not find an equalizer.

Manchester United ended their run of losing League Cup finals with an easy win over Wigan Athletic in 2006. Three second-half goals in the space of six minutes gave United a 4-0 win, only the second time that 4 goals have been scored in the final.

The 2007 final was between the youngsters of Arsenal and £150 million of talent from Chelsea, in the first all-London final. A keenly contested game was won for Chelsea with two goals by Drogba. The final moments were marred by three sendings off when tempers boiled over. This doubled at a stroke the sendings-off tally from previous finals. Toure and Adebayor of Arsenal and Mikel of Chelsea joined Andrei Kanchelskis (Manchester United, 1994), Justin Edinburgh (Spurs, 1999) and Clint Hill (Tranmere Rovers, 2000) in the record books.

Juande Ramos's Tottenham beat Avram Grant's Chelsea in the 2008 final and Spurs returned to the final in 2009, this time under Harry Rednapp's management. Their opponents were Manchester United. A low key final ended 0-0 after extra-time and even the kicks from the penalty mark were disappointing; United won the shoot-out 4-1. It was then United's turn to reach a second successive final, when they beat Aston Villa 2-1 in 2010.

Birmingham City and Arsenal met in the 2011 final. Birmingham's Ben Foster was "man of the match" for a string of saves in the second half, but Arsenal's keeper Szczesny was partly to blame for Birmingham's last minute winner from Martins.

THE ORGANISATION OF THE COMPETITION

With one exception in 1961/62, the competition has always consisted of 32 clubs at the third round stage. To cater for the number of clubs entering and those that are exempt until round three, different numbers of games have been played each season in rounds one and two. On one occasion (2002/03) the number of clubs exempt to round three meant that a single preliminary round tie was necessary to even up the number of clubs in round one.

In each season to 1995/96 some clubs were exempt until round two. The increased number of games that some clubs were playing in Europe led to the introduction of byes to round three from 1996/97 onwards.

All ties were single leg affairs at first, except for the semi-finals and final. Semi-finals continue to be played over two legs, but the final became a one-off event from 1966/67 onwards. Round one was played over two legs from 1975/76 to 2000/01 and round two was two-legged from 1979/80 to 2000/01.

Two-legged games that were level on aggregate after extra time in the second leg were replayed (as often as necessary) until 1974/75. Three ties went to a third replay in this period. Replays of two-legged games were settled by kicks from the penalty mark from 1975/76 onwards; a game at Hillsborough between Sheffield Wednesday and Darlington was the first to be decided this way. Replays of two-legged ties were abandoned in 1979-80 and the "away goals rule" or penalties (if the away goals were identical after extra time) used instead. Mansfield Town were the first successful club thanks to the away goals rule.

Single leg ties that were drawn continued to use as many replays as necessary; two other matches (in 1983/84 and 1989/90) needed three replays. Penalty kicks were used to settle the first replay from 1993/94 onwards.

Semi-final ties that were drawn on aggregate went to extra time; if still level, until 1986/87 they were replayed; i.e. the away goals rule was not used. Since then, the away goals rule and penalties have been used to settle the tie at the end of the second leg. The two-legged finals would have gone to a replay but one was never needed. When one-off finals were introduced, drawn games went to extra time and were then replayed until 1996/97, after which the penalty shoot out was introduced.

Seeding was introduced for the second round in season 1983/84. This means that round one winners are likely to be drawn against a club from a higher division. It also means that they are more likely to be knocked out of course!

The competition of 1961/62 did not follow the usual pattern. Leeds United were given a bye in round 3 and five clubs had a bye in round 4. They were Blackpool, Norwich City, Rochdale, Sheffield United and Sunderland.

Luton Town were drawn to play Cardiff City over two legs in round 2, 1986/87. Luton were refusing to allow away supporters to visit Kenilworth Road that season and consequently they were disqualified by the Football League. Cardiff City were given a bye.

ROLL OF HONOUR
(TO END 2010/11 SEASON)

Winners:

Seven times: Liverpool

Five times: Aston Villa

Four times: Chelsea, Manchester United, Nottingham Forest, Tottenham Hotspur

Three times: Leicester City

Twice: Arsenal, Birmingham City, Manchester City, Norwich City, Wolves

Once: Blackburn Rovers, Leeds United, Luton Town, Middlesbrough, Oxford United, Queen's Park Rangers, Sheffield Wednesday, Stoke City, Swindon Town, West Bromwich Albion

MEN OF THE MATCH

The Alan Hardaker Trophy has been awarded to the Man of the Match at every final since 1990. The winners are:

1990	Des Walker, Nottingham Forest
1991	Nigel Pearson, Sheffield Wednesday
1992	Brian McClair, Manchester United
1993	Paul Merson, Arsenal
1994	Kevin Richardson, Aston Villa
1995	Steve McManaman, Liverpool
1996	Andy Townsend, Aston Villa
1997	Steve Walsh, Leicester City
1998	Dennis Wise, Chelsea
1999	Allan Nielsen, Tottenham Hotspur
2000	Matt Elliott, Leicester City
2001	Robbie Fowler, Liverpool
2002	Brad Friedel, Blackburn Rovers
2003	Jerzy Dudek, Liverpool
2004	Boudewijn Zenden, Middlesbrough
2005	John Terry, Chelsea
2006	Wayne Rooney, Manchester United
2007	Didier Drogba, Chelsea
2008	Jonathon Woodgate, Tottenham Hotspur
2009	Ben Foster, Manchester United
2010	Antonio Valencia, Manchester United
2011	Ben Foster, Birmingham City

FOOTBALL LEAGUE CUP ALL TIME TABLE TO END 2010/11

Clubs are listed in order of games played
Games played on a neutral ground are counted as away games for both clubs

		home:					away:					
	p	w	d	l	f	a	w	d	l	f	a	perc
Aston Villa	221	75	18	16	247	95	54	25	33	188	160	58.37
Arsenal	206	77	15	15	219	77	42	25	32	157	123	57.77
Liverpool	205	71	20	9	248	86	50	22	33	167	111	59.02
West Ham United	198	72	16	16	246	90	32	21	41	125	148	52.53
Tottenham Hotspur	194	66	12	19	214	94	50	17	30	166	111	59.79
Norwich City	192	56	15	15	173	86	43	23	40	154	130	51.56
Manchester City	185	58	16	14	203	73	37	19	41	137	144	51.35
Birmingham City	185	56	14	23	181	104	32	23	37	117	140	47.57
Nottingham Forest	181	58	14	16	206	89	39	24	30	139	115	53.59
Southampton	176	56	16	14	182	88	25	27	38	117	123	46.02
Manchester United	173	63	11	11	179	74	36	17	35	122	118	57.23
Chelsea	173	50	14	14	158	84	38	20	37	152	126	50.87
Bolton Wanderers	173	49	14	24	162	115	30	19	37	121	154	45.66
Crystal Palace	173	49	19	16	173	84	29	17	43	94	135	45.09
Swindon Town	168	48	11	24	157	103	23	24	38	114	146	42.26
Blackburn Rovers	166	49	16	17	176	91	31	15	38	114	133	48.19
Rotherham United	165	44	16	25	144	104	26	13	41	89	145	42.42
Watford	164	44	21	20	162	100	28	9	42	97	132	43.90
Fulham	164	42	18	22	162	105	28	14	40	105	132	42.68
Ipswich Town	163	50	12	21	158	87	31	14	35	119	133	49.69
Tranmere Rovers	163	45	17	24	150	97	24	16	37	92	134	42.33
Burnley	162	42	10	27	135	100	30	18	35	117	141	44.44
Leicester City	161	42	14	15	130	83	38	13	39	127	129	49.69
Leeds United	161	47	12	28	154	101	30	11	33	112	112	47.83
Queen's Park Rangers	160	51	12	21	185	99	30	14	32	110	111	50.63
West Bromwich Albion	160	43	15	19	148	92	31	21	31	109	120	46.25
Middlesbrough	160	44	18	14	132	65	28	15	41	105	121	45.00
Stoke City	160	38	24	16	110	78	30	12	40	113	136	42.50
Sheffield Wednesday	159	44	15	17	150	86	34	16	33	120	115	49.06
Everton	159	41	16	20	162	78	36	17	29	123	93	48.43
Blackpool	159	46	16	18	154	95	19	17	43	88	145	40.88
Derby County	159	39	18	20	150	77	25	15	42	105	133	40.25
Portsmouth	157	44	15	18	131	79	23	15	42	100	143	42.68
Coventry City	154	48	10	18	162	90	30	11	37	103	132	50.65
Oxford United	154	45	20	17	148	94	25	14	33	78	99	45.45
Reading	153	38	19	21	135	94	22	16	37	97	139	39.22
Peterborough United	152	35	19	22	125	94	17	17	42	71	141	34.21
Sheffield United	151	52	11	17	155	78	17	14	40	84	135	45.70
Sunderland	150	41	12	23	139	98	25	17	32	104	119	44.00
Grimsby Town	147	43	17	18	128	77	16	12	41	60	117	40.14
Preston North End	147	33	15	20	106	78	24	15	40	93	150	38.78
Millwall	146	34	16	18	113	85	22	17	39	90	132	38.36
Bradford City	145	29	17	21	114	93	25	14	39	112	151	37.24
Luton Town	144	29	20	15	115	73	30	12	38	108	137	40.97
Huddersfield Town	144	28	17	20	95	79	24	16	39	101	135	36.11
Notts County	142	37	9	21	128	88	23	12	40	80	138	42.25
Bury	141	37	13	29	124	114	16	13	33	64	106	37.59
Barnsley	139	27	14	27	102	81	23	13	35	86	122	35.97
Bristol City	139	34	15	21	104	86	14	18	37	72	120	34.53
Northampton Town	138	29	15	20	99	73	18	12	44	74	137	34.06
Bournemouth	137	19	19	26	68	73	14	22	37	67	111	24.09
Walsall	136	26	15	20	83	78	24	9	42	90	128	36.76
Gillingham	136	28	14	23	97	83	16	11	44	60	133	32.35
Bristol Rovers	135	29	16	24	99	91	15	14	37	62	115	32.59
Charlton Athletic	134	34	8	24	119	84	19	15	34	88	126	39.55
Cardiff City	133	37	10	19	107	85	16	9	42	85	138	39.85

Continues over...

	home:						away:					
	p	w	d	l	f	a	w	d	l	f	a	perc
Brentford	133	31	11	24	99	94	9	13	45	70	146	30.08
Crewe Alexandra	131	32	15	23	107	94	13	12	36	76	134	34.35
Lincoln City	131	31	14	17	106	78	10	17	42	83	145	31.30
Stockport County	131	23	16	26	83	98	17	17	32	75	115	30.53
Brighton & Hove Albion	130	29	16	19	90	76	14	12	40	60	125	33.08
Plymouth Argyle	129	24	16	22	83	81	12	12	43	66	114	27.91
Oldham Athletic	128	30	10	13	116	80	17	10	48	59	138	36.72
Carlisle United	128	30	17	15	98	69	14	10	42	60	137	34.38
Wolverhampton Wan.	127	34	8	19	106	68	22	11	33	91	105	44.09
Newcastle United	126	34	5	19	110	63	22	10	36	88	111	44.44
Chesterfield	125	27	9	26	101	84	16	14	33	68	112	34.40
Shrewsbury Town	125	29	17	19	103	89	5	16	39	54	124	27.20
Swansea City	124	26	14	21	101	75	11	11	41	64	129	29.84
Leyton Orient	124	23	18	22	93	86	12	14	35	62	117	28.23
Southend United	122	28	12	19	74	69	13	11	39	69	133	33.61
Wrexham	121	21	13	25	83	94	18	9	35	68	127	32.23
Darlington	119	21	13	23	73	79	16	9	37	63	135	31.09
Hull City	119	26	12	20	78	75	9	10	42	62	134	29.41
York City	119	26	13	22	92	83	8	16	34	51	104	28.57
Scunthorpe United	119	24	14	28	85	91	7	12	34	38	107	26.05
Torquay United	117	16	12	32	63	86	11	17	29	62	108	23.08
Mansfield Town	116	22	11	26	82	90	12	11	34	77	132	29.31
Rochdale	116	20	9	27	83	98	8	12	40	55	126	24.14
Colchester United	115	25	9	24	95	80	11	7	39	55	113	31.30
Doncaster Rovers	115	27	12	23	96	105	7	15	31	52	115	29.57
Hartlepool United	115	22	14	19	81	79	9	7	44	53	144	26.96
Exeter City	115	17	15	26	74	93	12	12	33	54	111	25.22
Chester City	114	21	13	26	88	96	7	10	37	47	133	24.56
Port Vale	113	21	8	26	73	80	10	12	36	56	102	27.43
Wigan Athletic	100	28	6	19	79	57	12	7	28	52	88	40.00
Wimbledon	99	29	5	13	91	55	15	17	20	56	71	44.44
Cambridge United	87	17	13	12	56	53	8	6	31	42	90	28.74
Halifax Town	81	9	11	20	55	72	6	6	29	37	87	18.52
Hereford United	75	15	9	13	55	49	6	2	30	33	96	28.00
Aldershot	74	9	12	16	51	67	4	6	27	29	83	17.57
Newport County	64	13	7	13	48	45	4	7	20	34	72	26.56
Workington	49	9	8	6	34	18	11	3	12	39	54	40.82
Wycombe Wanderers	47	8	4	12	34	47	8	3	12	29	42	34.04
Scarborough	42	11	3	7	34	29	1	8	12	27	52	28.57
Barnet	37	8	5	3	29	21	4	1	16	21	53	32.43
Southport	35	4	6	7	24	26	6	0	12	17	32	28.57
Macclesfield Town	25	4	2	7	17	19	1	0	11	11	31	20.00
Barrow	22	6	2	4	17	16	0	2	8	10	34	27.27
Bradford Park Avenue	21	4	4	3	18	16	2	1	7	12	25	28.57
Cheltenham Town	18	3	0	4	13	12	2	1	8	9	23	27.78
Milton Keynes Dons	14	5	0	5	15	24	2	0	2	7	6	50.00
Yeovil Town	11	1	0	4	4	11	2	0	4	8	18	27.27
Accrington Stanley	10	2	0	2	5	5	1	0	5	6	10	30.00
Morecambe	7	1	0	1	3	3	2	0	3	6	16	42.86
Boston United	7	1	0	3	7	15	1	0	2	2	2	28.57
Rushden & Diamonds	7	1	0	2	0	4	1	0	3	4	15	28.57
Kidderminster Harriers	6	0	0	3	3	5	0	1	2	1	6	0.00
Maidstone United	6	0	1	2	2	4	0	0	3	2	10	0.00
Dagenham & Redbridge	4	0	0	2	2	4	0	0	2	2	5	0.00
Burton Albion	2	0	0	0	0	0	0	0	2	2	9	0.00
Stevenage	1	0	0	1	1	2	0	0	0	0	0	0.00

WEST HAM UNITED IN THE LEAGUE CUP

Summary of meetings: the year is the final year of the season, and West Ham's score is shown first.

Arsenal	1967	R3		3-1
Arsenal	1998	R5		1-2
Aston Villa	1962	R2		1-3
Aston Villa	1964	R3		2-0
Aston Villa	1989	R5		2-1
Aston Villa	1990	R3		0-0
Aston Villa	1990	R3	r	1-0
Aston Villa	1998	R3		3-0
Aston Villa	2000	R5		1-3
Barnet	1997	R2		1-1
Barnet	1997	R2s		1-0
Barnsley	1977	R2		3-0
Barnsley	1980	R2		3-1
Barnsley	1980	R2s		2-0
Barnsley	1981	R4		2-1
Barnsley	1988	R2		0-0
Barnsley	1988	R2s		2-5
Birmingham City	1990	R2		2-1
Birmingham City	1990	R2s		1-1
Birmingham City	2000	R4		3-2
Birmingham City	2011	SF1		2-1
Birmingham City	2011	SF2		1-3
Blackburn Rovers	2001	R3		2-0
Blackpool	1967	R5		3-1
Bolton Wanderers	1968	R3		4-1
Bolton Wanderers	1969	R2		7-2
Bolton Wanderers	1995	R4		1-3
Bolton Wanderers	2006	R3		0-1
Bolton Wanderers	2010	R3		1-3
Bournemouth	2000	R3		2-0
Bradford City	1992	R2		1-1
Bradford City	1992	R2s		4-0
Brighton & Hove Albion	1984	R3		1-0
Bristol City	1973	R2		2-1
Bristol City	1976	R2		0-0
Bristol City	1976	R2	r	3-1
Bristol City	1985	R2		2-2
Bristol City	1985	R2s		6-1
Bristol Rovers	1966	R2		3-3
Bristol Rovers	1966	R2	r	3-2
Bristol Rovers	1996	R2		1-0
Bristol Rovers	1996	R2s		3-0
Bristol Rovers	2008	R2		2-1
Burnley	1981	R2		2-0
Burnley	1981	R2s		4-0

Bury	1984	R2		2-1
Bury	1984	R2s		10-0
Cardiff City	1966	SF1		5-2
Cardiff City	1966	SF2		5-1
Cardiff City	1972	R2		1-1
Cardiff City	1972	R2	r	2-1
Cardiff City	2004	R2		3-2
Charlton Athletic	1961	R1		3-1
Charlton Athletic	1977	R3		1-0
Charlton Athletic	1981	R3		2-1
Chelsea	1995	R3		1-0
Chelsea	2005	R3		0-1
Chesterfield	1994	R2		5-1
Chesterfield	1994	R2s		2-0
Chesterfield	2003	R2		1-1
Chesterfield	2007	R3		1-2
Coventry City	1969	R3		0-0
Coventry City	1969	R3	r	2-3
Coventry City	1971	R3		1-3
Coventry City	1981	SF1		2-3
Coventry City	1981	SF2		2-0
Coventry City	2008	R4		2-1
Crewe Alexandra	1993	R2		0-0
Crewe Alexandra	1993	R2s		0-2
Darlington	1961	R2		2-3
Darlington	1976	R3		3-0
Derby County	1982	R2		3-2
Derby County	1982	R2s		2-0
Derby County	1989	R3		5-0
Derby County	1990	R5		1-1
Derby County	1990	R5	r	0-0
Derby County	1990	R5	r2	2-1
Everton	1984	R4		2-2
Everton	1984	R4	r	0-2
Everton	2008	R5		1-2
Fulham	1975	R3		1-2
Grimsby Town	1966	R5		2-2
Grimsby Town	1966	R5	r	1-0
Halifax Town	1970	R2		4-2
Huddersfield Town	1968	R4		0-2
Huddersfield Town	1998	R2		0-1
Huddersfield Town	1998	R2s		3-0
Hull City	1971	R2		1-0

Leeds United	1967	R4		7-0
Leeds United	1972	R3		0-0
Leeds United	1972	R3	r	1-0
Leicester City	1964	SF1		3-4
Leicester City	1964	SF2		0-2
Leyton Orient	1964	R2		2-1
Lincoln City	1983	R3		1-1
Lincoln City	1983	R3	r	2-1
Liverpool	1972	R4		2-1
Liverpool	1974	R2		2-2
Liverpool	1974	R2	r	0-1
Liverpool	1981	F		1-1
Liverpool	1981	F	r	1-2
Liverpool	1983	R5		1-2
Liverpool	1989	R4		4-1
Luton Town	1989	SF1		0-3
Luton Town	1989	SF2		0-2
Macclesfield Town	2009	R2		4-1
Manchester City	1985	R3		0-0
Manchester City	1985	R3	r	1-2
Manchester United	1986	R3		0-1
Manchester United	2011	R5		4-0
Mansfield Town	1966	R3		4-0
Millwall	2010	R2		3-1
Northampton Town	1999	R2		0-2
Northampton Town	1999	R2s		1-0
Norwich City	1992	R4		1-2
Nottingham Forest	1970	R3		0-1
Nottingham Forest	1978	R2		0-5
Nottingham Forest	1980	R5		0-0
Nottingham Forest	1980	R5	r	0-3
Nottingham Forest	1994	R3		1-2
Nottingham Forest	1997	R3		4-1
Notts County	1983	R4		3-3
Notts County	1983	R4	r	3-0
Notts County	2005	R2		3-2
Oldham Athletic	1990	SF1		0-6
Oldham Athletic	1990	SF2		3-0
Oldham Athletic	2003	R3		0-1
Oxford United	1987	R4		1-0
Oxford United	1991	R3		1-2
Oxford United	2011	R2		1-0
Plymouth Argyle	1962	R1		3-2
Plymouth Argyle	1963	R2		6-0
Plymouth Argyle	2008	R3		1-0

Preston North End	1987	R2		1-1
Preston North End	1987	R2s		4-1
Queen's Park Rangers	1977	R4		0-2
Reading	2002	R2		0-0
Rotherham United	1963	R3		1-3
Rotherham United	1966	R4		2-1
Rushden & Diamonds	2004	R1		3-1
Sheffield United	1972	R5		5-0
Sheffield United	1992	R3		2-0
Sheffield Wednesday	2001	R4		1-2
Sheffield Wednesday	2006	R2		4-2
Southampton	1996	R3		1-2
Southend United	1980	R3		1-1
Southend United	1980	R3	r	0-0
Southend United	1980	R3	r2	5-1
Southend United	2005	R1		2-0
Stockport County	1973	R3		1-2
Stockport County	1997	R4		1-1
Stockport County	1997	R4	r	1-2
Stoke City	1972	SF1		2-1
Stoke City	1972	SF2		0-1
Stoke City	1972	SFR	r	0-0
Stoke City	1972	SFR	r2	2-3
Stoke City	1983	R2		1-1
Stoke City	1983	R2s		2-1
Stoke City	1991	R2		3-0
Stoke City	1991	R2s		2-1
Stoke City	2011	R4		3-1
Sunderland	1965	R2		1-4
Sunderland	1980	R4		1-1
Sunderland	1980	R4	r	2-1
Sunderland	1989	R2		3-0
Sunderland	1989	R2s		2-1
Sunderland	2011	R3		2-1
Swansea City	1986	R2		3-0
Swansea City	1986	R2s		3-2
Swindon Town	1964	R4		3-3
Swindon Town	1964	R4	r	4-1
Swindon Town	1979	R2		1-2
Tottenham Hotspur	1967	R2		1-0
Tottenham Hotspur	1976	R4		0-0
Tottenham Hotspur	1976	R4	r	0-2
Tottenham Hotspur	1981	R5		1-0
Tottenham Hotspur	1987	R5		1-1
Tottenham Hotspur	1987	R5	r	0-5
Tottenham Hotspur	2004	R3		0-1

Tranmere Rovers	1975	R2		0-0
Tranmere Rovers	1975	R2	r	6-0
Walsall	1968	R2		5-1
Walsall	1995	R2		1-2
Walsall	1995	R2s		2-0
Walsall	1998	R4		4-1
Walsall	2001	R2		1-0
Walsall	2001	R2s		1-1
Watford	1987	R3		3-2
Watford	2009	R3		0-1
West Bromwich Albion	1966	F1		2-1
West Bromwich Albion	1966	F2		1-4
West Bromwich Albion	1967	SF1		0-4
West Bromwich Albion	1967	SF2		2-2
West Bromwich Albion	1982	R3		2-2
West Bromwich Albion	1982	R3	r	1-1
West Bromwich Albion	1982	R3	r2	0-1
Wimbledon	1990	R4		1-0
Workington	1964	R5		6-0